DO ANYTHING

FAN PODCASTING:
THE COMPLETE GUIDE

by Bill Meeks

Published by Do Anything Media
http://doanything.media
Cover artwork designed by Bill Meeks.

ISBN-13: 9798613479405

Contents

Acknowledgements

I couldn't have written this book without the input of the many podcasters quoted throughout. Big thanks to all of you.

Thanks to my beta readers for providing a ton of great feedback on every aspect of the book. They are Anne Marie DeSimone, Hope Mullinax, Rebecca Johnson, Wynn Mercere, Elizabeth Plascencia, Nathan Beatty, Bobby "from Bradenton" Hawke, Holly Mac, Morgan Glennon, Monica Jones, Derek O'Neill, and Tracy Comeau.

Finally, thanks to everybody who listened. Without your kind attention over the years, I wouldn't know enough to write this book.

Foreword - Who The Heck Are You, And Why Should I Care?

My name is Bill Meeks, and for seven years I hosted "fancasts" with my partner Anne Marie DeSimone. We started in an unheated garage with a handheld bi-directional recorder, and within two years we were live streaming three nights a week with pro microphones, a modest set, props, and an active chat room calling us out whenever we got something wrong. We made money too. Not enough to live on, but more than enough to fund everything and put a few dollars in our pocket.

At the height of our Universe Box podcast network, we were getting 40,000 unique downloads a month across several shows. Our first hit was *Greetings From Storybrooke*, where we talked about the ABC TV series *Once Upon A Time*. Our most popular show, *Legends of Gotham*, covered the Fox series Gotham, set in the world of Batman. By most measurements, we were the top Gotham podcast, although I always thought the *Gotham TV Podcast* did a better job. For a few years, we were killing it. We formed relationships with the people making the shows. We built a kind, generous, and creative community. Most importantly, we had a heck of a lot of fun doing it.

I've thought a lot about what it takes to discuss a show every week, even when you aren't feeling it. I've thought a lot about criticism, and I found a way to review a show that won't piss off all your listeners. I've spent a lot of time, both in podcasting and for big media companies, building and growing creative communities online, and I have some thoughts on how to do it effectively.

This book isn't a technical guide on how to record great audio, build a podcast feed, monetize your show, etc. There are already many great resources that cover those topics. I recommend *The Audacity to Podcast,* from my fellow Once-caster Daniel J. Lewis, to learn more about the technical side of podcasting. You don't need a tech guide from me. I know things about audio, but I'm not an audio expert. I don't care which mic stand you buy. I don't know how to get a MeUndies promo code deal. Content is king. I'm an expert in fancasting and community building, so that's the book I'm writing.

> *"Everybody can podcast, and you can podcast about anything you want to."* Stephanie Smith, Host - **PotentialCast: A Buffy The Vampire Slayer Podcast**

I know a lot of other podcasters who create content based on popular movies, TV shows, books, etc. You'll see them chime in[1] throughout the book, offering a fresh perspective on the topic that, in many cases, I disagree with. And that's okay. For most of this stuff, there is no

---

[1] Some quotations came from a survey I sent out while researching this book, and from my fancasting beta readers. Some came from my new interview show I Made This. I've also pulled quotes from a panel I hosted at Dragon Con in 2013 called How To Start A Fancast. You can listen to the full panel here: http://links.doanything.media/fanpodcastpanel

one "right" answer. There is the "right" answer for you, the one that helps you create compelling content about the things you love. I hope between my opinions, the opinions of my friends, and your own podcast preferences, you'll triangulate a formula that sets you up for success.

"Criticism should have standards. That way, if you're using those same standards every single time, you can judge everything fairly." Rebecca Johnson, Host - **Supergirl Radio**

Our listeners always liked how fair we were when reviewing shows, movies, or whatever. Even when we didn't like something, we approached it with fairness and positivity. Sure, we spilled the occasional bucket of Haterade on a dumpster fire, but we tried to give anything we reviewed a fair shake. It wasn't an accident. We succeeded thanks to our patented critical process. To be fair, we didn't come up with it. It started with a dude named Johann Wolfgang von Goethe.

Goethe outlined three criteria for theatrical criticism that I learned when studying theater in college and totally ripped off. Keeping these questions in mind when you put together your podcast each week will ensure your review remains objective, but with a healthy dose of your personal opinion to add some flavor.

What was done?
How well was it done?
Was it worth doing?

For this example, I'm reviewing an episode of PAW Patrol, the hit kid show that turned adorable puppies into hardened police dogs. While it's easy to dismiss the show's bland plots and problematic premise out of hand, if you ask yourself Goethe's questions, you'll still deliver a fair and positive review.

PAW Podtrolls Podcast Episode #1 - "Rocky And Rubble Are The Same Dog"

What was done? Spin Master and Nickelodeon designed a show to demonstrate the value of thoughtful problem-solving. The puppies needed to be cute, and the show needed to appeal to preschoolers.

How well was it done? This is where your personal opinion starts to come into play. Keep your answer to the first question in mind.

When considering what was done, or the goals of the project, PAW Patrol was done well. While I find the entire show and most of the characters grating, PAW Patrol delivers cute puppies solving problems, with competent animation and sound design.

Was it worth doing? Well, the show is still running and has sold a ton of toys, so Nickelodeon is happy. But as an educational work of art? That's up to you. Using your previous two answers, determine if PAW Patrol was worth the manpower required to make it, not for the studio, but for the people watching it. You know, the people listening to your podcast. In my opinion, PAW Patrol hit the nail on the head and is watchable, even if I'd never willingly choose to watch it. If you're a toddler looking to learn, or a dog lover looking to laugh at dad jokes, this is the show for you.

"You have to meet the work of art where it is, not where you want it to be." Morgan Glennon, Host - Supergirl Radio/Legends of Tomorrow Podcast

So there we have it... A comprehensive review of PAW Patrol that acknowledges the work for what it is, addresses the flaws, and finds a lens to view kid stuff in a positive, mature light. You probably even know my personal opinion about the show, and I wasn't a big jerk about not liking it, either.

Too often, reviews are more about the author's ego than the work itself. Too many reviews focus on the reviewer, and how they could have done a better job making the thing they're reviewing. Most wouldn't make something better than the professionals they criticize. Coming in with a vendetta is disrespectful to the fans who listen to your show. Most of them love that thing you're dousing in Haterade. If you can't disagree with them respectfully, they aren't going to download your podcast.

"I know, every week, I can find something I really like." Les Howard, Host - The Signal

As a critic, you should hold yourself to a higher standard. The criteria I stole from Goethe via my college professor will help you deliver even the most negative criticism in an objective, positive way. I'm not saying you shouldn't share your opinion. Far from it! You can say anything you want as long as your listeners think you're fair.

After all, that's who we're doing this for, right? The listeners? Not ourselves? Good. Just checking.

"It can be more work than you realize. There's a fandom out there that is hopefully as rabid as you are. There are times, with network release schedules and things going on in your personal life, that the (host) is not there for the fans, and you need to be prepared for that. But if you can be there, if you can meet those demands, it can be extremely rewarding. There's a lot of work that goes into it, but the work pays off in the engagement of the fans." Darrell Darnell, Co-Founder - **Golden Spiral Media**.

L ike any other medium, you'll need passion and drive to create great content. When I started

Greetings From Storybrooke, it was because I genuinely liked ABC's *Once Upon A Time* and wanted to share my opinions. I made it for selfish reasons, at first.

> "I podcast for myself first and foremost, because I love doing it. It helped me find my identity as a queer woman, and I've used it to find my voice. If I didn't do it for me first, then I would have given up before I ever got my first comment." Hope Mullinax, **Jaig Eyes And Jedi, Geeky Girl Experience**.

It is perfectly fine to create a podcast for selfish reasons. Thousands of people do it every day, and some of them find great success, but the ones that succeed all do one thing right: They care about their listeners.

What do we, as fancasters, owe to our listeners? What do they get from our shows, and what can we do to keep them coming back? To figure it out, we'll need to mosey on down to the *Café POV*.

C.A.F.E.P.O.V. is an acronym that lays out the **seven things we owe our listeners**.

- Consistency
- Accuracy
- Friendship
- Expansion
- Play
- Objectivity
- Voice

You know, the *Café POV*. Remember that feeling back in college, when you'd gather around a table with a bunch of friends from class and talk about your favorite bands? Those late nights at summer camp where you'd theorize about your favorite movies with the lights out? *That's* the *Café POV*. That feeling of connection and companionship... That feeling is what we owe our listeners.

Through the hundreds of episodes I've recorded, I've developed techniques to foster the *Café POV*. If you build these seven concepts into your show, you'll form a deep connection with your listeners and create content they'll care about.

Let's step through these one at a time.

Consistency

> "You have to feed the beast. If you do that kind of thing, if you have an audience, you have to feed them. You have to give them what they want, or give them what they need, or direct them to what they need. And you can't let them go. You don't ever take them for granted. Don't expect that just because they were there for you on Friday night they'll still be there for you on Monday morning." - **Rich Johnston, Head Writer/Founder, Bleeding Cool**

Consistency is important, more so when you're building a podcast around somebody else's schedule. The networks generally air their shows on the same day, at the same time, every week. Movie studios announce a movie two years in advance, and almost always hit the release date. So too, should you aim to release your podcast on a consistent schedule. As Rich Johnson said, your listeners are fickle. In an age of nearly infinite entertainment options, even your biggest fans will be put off if you release your podcast covering the season finale two days or a week after they watched it. At that point, their busy fan brains are already theorizing about what comes next, or reading Alternate Universe fanfics involving a Riverdale/Pretty Little Liars/Spongebob crossover.

"I make sure to tweet and post on Facebook to let listeners know that it's coming a little bit later than usual and most people seem okay with that. But, listeners do notice when it's not up yet."
Rebecca Johnson, Host - Supergirl Radio

It was important to me that we release our podcasts within 28 hours of a show airing, a glacial pace compared to modern standards. It was just enough time to properly prepare and talk to your fans while they were still excited about the episode.

I get it. Life happens, and a lot of us aren't getting paid for this. If you miss a publish date and see your schedule slipping, don't give up. Odds are, the listeners who were excited to hear your take on the latest Olicity[2] drama Wednesday morning will be just as excited to hear it Thursday morning. The important thing is to acknowledge the inconsistency, let your listeners know you regret it, then take steps to ensure it never happens again.

I always offered a little "value add" if we were late. We'd either do an extra-long episode, or stick around in the chat room after we wrapped our live stream to talk with the listeners.

---

[2] **Olicity** refers to the relationship, between the characters Oliver and Felicity on the CW show *Arrow*, a huge source of controversy in the *Arrow* fandom and a running joke with some of my friends over at DCTV Podcasts.

When you're a podcaster, you become a routine for the people who listen to your show. You're as important to their Wednesday as that first cup of coffee after they get out of the shower. If you aren't there when they come looking, you'd better make *damned* sure you make it up to them. You're always building a relationship with your listeners, whether you know it or not. Don't strain that relationship without a good reason, and make it up to them when you do.

Accuracy

> "Re-immersing myself in the material I'm reviewing is an important part, but the fundamental component to preparation is writing notes on the areas I'll be analyzing. I don't have a problem with doing analysis off the cuff, which I do every episode, but because of my tendency to 'waffle on' about certain topics that I have a lot of ideas (but no structured points) about, it is ideal to just write down what I'm targeting and what conclusion I'm trying to get to." - Jamal , Host - **Get In The Mecha**

You can't remember everything that happens. A network show has more than twenty episodes a season... You're going to forget things, often, even things that happened in the episode you're reviewing!

> "Make a mistake. Call a character the wrong name, and they'll flood into the inbox." Kevin Bachelder, Host - **Tuning Into SciFi TV**

Your audience, as a collective, remembers every moment perfectly. Every line, every nuanced piece of continuity, every sliver of foreshadowing. They'll notice when you're wrong, and they'll usually call you out on it.

Don't freak out! Your listeners will forgive the occasional error, provided they hear you come into every podcast prepared to inform and entertain them. We have an entire chapter later on weekly preparation, so it's a pretty big deal. A solid "Show Doc" will up your accuracy, augment your faulty memory, and set you apart from the majority of new podcasters who ramble and fall down rabbit holes and 'waffle on' about everything but the show they promised their listeners they'd discuss.

> "I'm very upfront about my faulty memory and I rely on (my co-host, Rebecca) to help me out, as she's the organized one in our duo. But anytime a listener writes in to point something out, we always give that person all the props." Morgan Glennon, Host - Supergirl Radio/Legends of Tomorrow Podcast

The reasons people listen to fancasts in the first place are to understand a story more completely, or reaffirm their own opinions, or get another perspective on something they love. If you want them to commit to a standing date with you every week, you can't half-ass it.

Know your shit, and your audience will forgive your inevitable mistakes.

Pro Tip: Shine a spotlight on a listener when they call you out. Don't shame them, or criticize them for correcting you. Praise them. Build them up into a community celebrity. If somebody cares enough to correct you, they must care about your podcast an awful lot. As a good host, you should elevate them and make them feel important. Your other listeners will see this, and they'll be encouraged to contribute. Before you know it, maybe you'll end up like us and have so much feedback you'll have to do special episodes just to get to all of it.

Friendship

> "You go to see the band that you're friends with, you know? You go to see (your) friend that's in the band." - Michael Dolce , Host - **Secrets of the Sire**

The hardest part about meeting new friends is introducing yourself. When you host a podcast, you introduce yourself to new people every episode. Your audience listens to you, attentively, for hours a month. They probably know a lot about you already. Bare minimum, they know your personality, your sense of humor, and your general take on the subject matter. When they talk back, the conversation can get real personal, real quick. In most cases, that's great! It means you're attracting "ride-or-die" friends you can count on to help your show in a variety of ways.

Count on fans-turned-friends to offer up honest feedback on your podcast, an invaluable asset as you hone your craft. Since you've taken the time to build a genuine friendship, the criticism is always constructive and can only make your show better.

If you include listener feedback in your podcast, and you *should*, your listeners will make bold choices, sending e-mails in-character as Oswald Cobblepot or leaving voicemails as The Joker. This is great, and rewards the other fans who listen every week.

"Community involvement is huge in what we do. We had a Fringe finale party. I live in Oklahoma City, it's not exactly a Mecca of the world, and in the middle of January, we had fifty people from the US and Canada come in and watch the finale with us. It's all because of the community we established around **The Fringe Podcast**. We all have this passion of geeky television shows and sci-fi and really well-done TV. The community is so important to what we do. It's the most important thing we do, really." Darrell Darnell, Co-Founder - Golden Spiral Media

Me and Anne Marie meeting up with listeners Josh Phelps and Eric Hansen at Disney World.

Many of my listeners have been to my house, or slept on my couch, or told me how much they loved the podcast when they saw my *Greetings From Storybrooke* t-shirt at Disney World. They've confided in me, given me solid advice, and supported my other projects. When you have time, support their creative projects too. It's always an honor when a listener asks you for feedback on their first podcast or book.

Expansion

> "I wanted something live, something that could grow, something I could keep plussing with ideas, you see? The park means a lot to me in that it's something that will never be finished. Something that I can keep developing, keep plussing and adding to. It's alive. It will be a live, breathing thing that will need changes." - Walt Disney

Never be satisfied with your show. Sitting down to record should never feel boring. While I'll get into the importance of structure in a later chapter, shaking things up keeps your audience engaged. They'll never be sure which delightful surprise you'll spring on them next.

When we reviewed "Suicide Squad" on Legends of Gotham, we got into character.

When we started live streaming our podcasts on YouTube, it opened up tons of options for what I call "specials," cool or interesting things you can change up each week. Recording on Halloween? Dress up in costume. Did the show you're reviewing have a musical episode? Why don't you sing the episode summary? Add a countdown of your favorite one-liners in the middle of the episode. Play a surprise voicemail from a cast member. Pretend an unpopular episode didn't happen, with a wink to the audience to let them know you know you're wrong.

LEGENDS OF GOTHAM #25
S01E16 "The Blind Fortune Teller"

We would redecorate our set for every stream. For "Legends of Gotham," we added 25 unique set decorations, including a signed picture from Renee Montoya actress Victoria Cartagena.

Those are just some ideas, all of which we did. Feel free to steal them, but I think you'll find more success developing your own specials. Only you know your show's voice, and what your listeners will appreciate and tolerate. These are value-adds. Make sure, however you decide to expand your podcast, that it benefits the listener.

Play

"No one looks stupid when they're having fun." -
Amy Poehler

In improv comedy, you create entertaining scenes by
entering into "radical agreement" with your scene
partner. If they say you've been hiking for six hours,
move and act like somebody who's been hiking for six
hours. Don't block them by bouncing around the stage,
screaming that it's only been ten minutes. Agree with
what they say, then add to or expand on it. Above all else,
make the other person look good, and trust that they'll
do the same for you. You'll create a playful environment.
You know, play? What you used to do out on the
playground at recess? Cops and robbers? Fortnite? I can't
tell how old you are through the page.

Podcast co-hosts should enter into a covenant of
radical agreement. Two people are bound to have
different opinions. That's fine. Don't shy away from those
conversations.

Disagree without being disagreeable. You might think
your co-host is dead wrong about the over-saturation of
the Olicity 'ship[3] on *Arrow*, but you can argue your point

---

[3] **'Ship**, short for romantic relationship, a term
popularized in fanfiction circles. Often, discussing 'ships
involves owning a relationship between characters by
labeling it as your "One True Pairing," or **OTP**. "Shipping

without attacking theirs. Like it or not, all your co-hosts are beloved characters to your listeners. If you turn on each other, you'll break a lot of hearts. Always make your co-hosts look good.

> "Being able to respectfully disagree with someone comes down to, 'Do I value this person?' If you truly care about the other person, you are going to listen to what they have to say and make every effort to be thoughtful in your response. The other person will feel that and pay it back to you in kind. Don't put the other person's back up against the wall. Invite them to engage in (a conversation)." Rebecca Johnson, Host - Supergirl Radio

Accept their offers, even if you disagree with them. Let them know you understand their point of view, then add to or expand on it. Maybe there's an aspect of Olicity's relationship that makes you physically ill. Maybe you think slash fiction focusing on the Toliver[4] 'ship is a bigger issue. Maybe you came up with a great Lauriver joke. Just keep playing. Keep having fun.

Don't sink your podcast over a 'ship.

---

culture" in fandoms is both wonderful and toxic to fan communities. If you keep a sense of play when discussing 'ships, your listeners should react in a positive way, even if they have another OTP.

[4] Another 'ship from *Arrow*. Don't ask me about it though. I had to look another Arrow example up.

Objectivity

> "I think perfect objectivity is an unrealistic goal;
> fairness, however, is not." - Michael Pollan

As discussed in the previous chapter covering Goethe's three questions, it's important to present your opinion in an objective way. If you have a conclusion, explain to your listeners how you arrived at that conclusion. Show them the logic behind your opinion. They'll respect you, even if they disagree.

Voice

> "Become established as the place to go to for fans. Share their fan art and ask for their thoughts. If the fans don't want to listen, you won't have an audience." - Derek O'Neill, **TV Podcast Industries**

> "Everybody wants to be somebody fancy. Even if they're shy." - Donald Miller

At some point, every single one of your listeners has considered starting their own podcast, if they haven't done it already. Some people don't have the self-confidence. Others don't have the time, or the technical know-how.

These people are your show's greatest assets.

If somebody cares enough about something to listen to an hour-long podcast about it, odds are they have a lot of their own opinions. Every fancaster should monitor fan reactions online. What better way to do that than to solicit them from your listeners? Give your viewers multiple ways to contribute to your show over voicemail, e-mail, social media, Tik Tok, whatever. Feature their contributions. Make them feel like a star.

> "If ten people respond to anything on the internet, that is really rad. It's like you just got ten new friends." Justin Robert Young, Host - Who's The Boss?

I tried to not leave any feedback out of the show, but sometimes it wasn't possible to read every letter or play every voicemail without adding two hours to our podcast. Consider publishing a blog on your website, or create a social post to respond to a question in more detail.

> "There will be episodes the listeners will pick apart, but it's their passion, and they see no flaws. But wouldn't you rather they be honest?" Stephanie Smith, Host - PotentialCast: A Buffy The Vampire Slayer Podcast

For the feedback you do include, maintain that same radical agreement you share with your co-host. Never shame or belittle somebody brave enough to share a piece of themselves with you and their fellow listeners, or you'll run out of listeners quick.

Yes, there are trolls out there. Most people think trolls are your enemy, but I think of them more as fans who aren't ready to admit it yet. See the chapter on dealing with trolls for my thoughts on how to convert them into your most committed listeners.

If you build your podcast with a *Café POV,* your podcast will be entertaining, sustainable, and inclusive. Your listeners will love you, your numbers will climb, and you'll attract a community of like-minded friends. You might even get a few of them to buy you a cup of coffee.

"The structure of the podcast tends to be very produced, very scripted. There are different segments. We know what's going to be spliced in where, but we try really hard not to be too scripted so that it just comes across like us talking." Les Howard, Host - The Signal

P icking a format makes your show more consistent. You want to find a good structure to start with, one that you can adapt and modify as the podcast grows. There are several common components that most fancasts use. Pick some you like, combine them with your own original segment ideas, then organize them into a Show Doc, which we'll discuss later.

Common Fancasts Segments

Plot Summary

A brief reminder of the show or movie you're reviewing. Keep it short and sweet. If somebody listens to your podcast reviewing a thing, odds are they watched the thing, so you don't need to offer a beat-by-beat breakdown of the thing right up front. Feel free to summarize key events as they come up in the main discussion, but most listeners have everything fresh in their minds already. This should be, at most, a reminder. Too many fancasts spend 15 minutes or more summarizing the episode, when 30 seconds is more than enough.

This is a great place to let your creativity shine. I wrote rhyming episode summaries, like this one for the *Once Upon A Time* episode "Darkness on the Edge of Town":

> The Spice Girls of Evil are helping the Dark One.
> Their plan for redemption is a cleverly stark one:
> Hunt down The Author and give him some notes.
> Take the bad stuff, but leave the fur coats.
> Storybrooke's moved on from their Frozen folly,
> minus the scroll which still serves as a trolley.
> Chernabog's looking for somebody evil. Does the
> Savior he hunts even come from good people?
> *Once* has returned. It's time to get down. Let's
> get lost in the *Darkness on the Edge of Town.*

I mention key plot points (the bad guys team up and enact a plan, something carries over from the Frozen arc, etc.), drop in a running joke from the podcast (Spice Girls of Evil), then get on with the discussion our listeners came to hear.

Writing a new rhyme every week was a fun challenge. Whenever I got stuck, I'd turn to RhymeZone.com for assistance. You can search for rhymes, organized by part of speech or syllable count. You can even search for near rhymes or slant rhymes that give you more options when you're trying to find a good rhyme for "orange." Porridge? Door hinge? Lawrence? Orange Lawrence. I kind of like that. Anyway, it's a good site.

RhymeZone also serves up synonyms, antonyms, and a reverse dictionary. It's a great reference site if you're a writer, even if you aren't writing poems for your podcast.

Main Discussion

> *"They need a spirit guide to walk them through the show."* Stephanie Smith, Host - PotentialCast: A Buffy The Vampire Slayer Podcast

This is the meat of the episode. I broke it up into two sections to give the hosts a breather, but many podcasters keep it all together.

There are a couple of approaches here. Do a free-form discussion based around key plot points, or have each host come up with a list of topics they'd like to talk about, before opening things up for a group discussion. If you go with the second option, take turns so nobody dominates too much of the conversation.

You'll see how we organized our discussion points in our sample Show Doc.

Overall Rating

> "We'll give ratings for each of our shows. Things like 'Watch It Now' or 'Watch It Soon.' When the listeners hear our opinions are divergent, the listeners are like 'Ooh, can't wait to hear them talk about that' because it's very different. But we won't force it by taking different sides. If it's natural, great." Kevin Bachelder, Host - Tuning Into SciFi TV

Once you wrap up your discussion, it's a good idea to summarize your feelings in some quantifiable way. It puts a cap on the discussion, and oftentimes will get the listeners back on your side if you went too negative.

We used to do something called an "arbitrary scale." I would combine a random number with a random thing from the episode, then we'd both rate it on the scale and allow our chat room to weigh in with their ratings.

For example, in the Season 2 episode of *Gotham* titled "Unleashed," Theo Galavan, a villain, is shot with a rocket launcher by Penguin. Hence, my arbitrary scale for the episode was "272 Globs of Galavan." Our live viewers would often suggest arbitrary scales during the recording. Revealing the scale each week made the chat room explode with surprise and delight.

You might prefer a more consistent rating metric. Stars or thumbs up/down or A-B-C grades. However you rate the episode, always err on the high side when picking your rating. If the show hits a rough patch and you dislike several episodes in a row, consistently low ratings will anger your listeners who are still enjoying the series.

When you justify your rating, keep things positive. I would generally pick three reasons I liked it, and maybe one reason I didn't, but only if I felt pretty strongly about it. You can go negative without serious consequences if the overall fan consensus is negative, but be careful. The one person who liked the episode might be the same person you get an awesome voicemail from every week.

News

In today's anti-spoiler culture, this section can be tricky. You should report on big announcements and rumors, but you don't want to spoil key plot points for your listeners. When *Once Upon A Time* or *Gotham* went on hiatus, we'd often do a special Spoiler Party episode to speculate on all the big news.

> "We break our show into two halves. The first half is what we call the 'Water Cooler,' and that is spoiler free. We tell folks that. There are some folks who are sensitive to casting news, so we will say we have some casting news coming up. Then we have the back half of the show we call 'The Back Porch,' and we tell people if they listen to that part, be prepared for there not to be any spoiler warnings." Kevin Bachelder, Host - Tuning Into SciFi TV

If you're going to get into spoiler territory in your news section, put it as late in your podcast as possible, so your listeners get the most value out of your podcast before they have to turn it off. You might think you can ask them to skip ahead, but that's a pain and a lot of users will just bounce. Make it clear you'll be discussing spoilers. Say it plain: "If you don't want spoilers about (the thing), stop listening." Don't be cute with it, because cute is confusing and the last thing you want is to ruin a listener's experience with an unclear spoiler warning.

> "We stopped doing spoilers because, you know, I don't want to be spoiled as a fan. The one thing we'd do is episode titles, which some people do consider a spoiler. I do think if you're going to feel spoiled by a title, you need to get over it." Les Howard, Host - The Signal

During the run of *Gotham*, two lead actors had a tabloid moment. We struggled with how to cover it in the News section. It was everywhere online, so we had to address it, but we didn't want to sit in judgment on the actors or their personal choices. We didn't aim to be the TMZ of fancasts. Maybe you do, but I'd advise against it. If you do want to go the gossip route, that's fine, but its a decision you should make in the planning stages before you launch your podcast.

Making snarky comments about an actor's personal life might seem fun or funny in the moment, but people don't come to you for hot gossip. They come to hear you discuss the characters, themes, and plot of their favorite piece of fiction. Save your critical voice for the content of whatever it is you're reviewing. If a story like this breaks, inform your listeners, then move on. What if you get the opportunity to interview the actor? You don't want a clip where you speculate on their birth control habits floating around, right?

History Lessons

One of your jobs as a fancaster is to educate and inform your listeners about the influences behind the show or movie you're discussing. Especially for shows based on popular properties like comic books or novels, you want to position yourself as a subject matter expert. For

Gotham, any time they introduced a character from the comics, I'd devote at least one of my discussion points to teaching the listeners about that character's history.

"Start planning as early as you can. We had ten episodes out before the show even aired one." - Derek O'Neill, TV Podcast Industries

"If none of us are familiar with the source material, we will have a guest on to explain the character or storyline to us." Morgan Glennon, Host - Supergirl Radio/Legends of Tomorrow Podcast

While we folded history lessons into the main discussion, many podcasters devote a segment to explaining the lore to new fans. My friends over at DCTV Podcasts devote a dozen or more episodes to character history, often launching their podcast as soon as the show is announced by the network. These "Year Zero" specials grab potential listeners early, establish you as the expert, and make your show more visible when people search for a podcast after watching the series premiere. When they hit your feed, you'll have tons of content waiting for them. When they binge your history lesson episodes, it will boost your numbers and make your show easier to find.

Listener Feedback

> "Don't expect the first time you (ask for feedback), that everybody is going to flood in there and do it. You have to keep asking, every week." Kevin Bachelder, Host - Tuning Into SciFi TV

Including listener feedback is crucial to the success of your show. It's social proof that you aren't just a madman with a microphone, spitting your thoughts into the void. As discussed in our chapter on the *Café POV* mindset, your listeners want to be part of the show. Make it easy for them to weigh in.

> *"If you aren't getting feedback, ask a specific question."* Stephanie Smith, Host - PotentialCast: A Buffy The Vampire Slayer Podcast

There is a danger here. You need to keep the feedback segment moving, or listeners are likely to tune out early. If you have the time, consider trimming down voicemails[5] in Audacity, or editing e-mails down to one or two key points. Bottom line, unless it's a special occasion like an all-feedback episode or a season finale discussion,

---

[5] Just make sure you don't edit them down so much that you end up misrepresenting the listner's opinion. Edit, don't remix.

feedback shouldn't take up more than ten to fifteen percent of your total run time.

If you cut feedback for time, find some way to let people know you read it. Shout out the listeners you didn't have time for at the end of the segment, or post a blog on your website with feedback you couldn't get to on the podcast. Even when somebody's feedback doesn't make the show, they shouldn't feel like it was a wasted effort. You want engagement. Make sure you reward any engagement you get, even if you can't fit it into the podcast.

While we saved listener feedback for the end of the episode, I always liked including one e-mail or voicemail in the middle of the main discussion. It gives you a little breather where you don't have to think and/or talk, and it gives listeners who shut the podcast off after the main discussion a taste of what they're missing.

Reoccurring Segment

Create a branded reoccurring segment that appears in all or most of your episodes. My friends over at *Supergirl Radio* love Lena Luthor's fashion sense, so much so that they discuss her fashion choices almost every week. They also have a running gag about how Snapper Carr never snaps.

When *Gotham* premiered, there was a lot of speculation about how and when the Joker would show up. Executive Producer John Stephens said there would be many possible Jokers introduced, but that they might never get around to revealing who it actually was. We knew this would be something our listeners would be looking out for, so we introduced a segment called *Look At This Joker*, where we called out any potential Jokers, references to the Joker, or general Joker chatter circling the show. We'd start with an improvised theme song, then dive in with our thoughts and theories. This also gave me an opportunity to further educate the listeners about the various versions of the Joker through the years, so that when Ace Chemical Plant showed up, our listeners spotted it immediately. We also compiled notes on every "Look At This Joker" segment onto a page of our web site, which garnered us thousands of hits every month from *Gotham* fans researching their own Joker theories.

Whatever reoccurring segment you decide to go with, make sure it's sustainable. When we brought back *Legends of Gotham* for the final season, the Jeremiah character was Joker in everything but name, so we had to create a new branded segment, "Light The Knight," which never quite worked as well. Consider waiting until later in Season 1 to establish a reoccurring segment, so you can feel out the tropes of the show and find a topic with staying power.

Creating A Show Doc

Now that you know what segments you'll include in your show, it's time to organize them into a template, or Show Doc, you and your co-hosts can work from to plan your podcast every week. I suggest using a collaborative editor like Google Docs, so that everybody involved can add their notes as needed. This also helps you reorganize the show, or cut a segment if the podcast is running long, without having to say anything about it on-mic.

> "If you create your notes about an episode or whatever thing you're reviewing in Google Docs, (you'll have) a search engine for future reference. I have been able to pull some random quote or factoid from an episode seasons ago because I took the time to make detailed notes when the episode aired." Rebecca Johnson, Host - Supergirl Radio

I've seen many different types of Show Docs. Some people like spreadsheets. I always favored a basic bullet point outline. We have an actual example[6] from one of our Legends of Gotham episodes. You might find it hard to follow, as it turned into a Frankenstein document over the years, but this is the basic format:

---

[6] http://links.doanything.media/sampleshowdoc

I. - Opening - *"Custom line pulled from the most recent episode."* Welcome to Legends of Gotham, where we talk about Fox's hit series GOTHAM, set in the world of Batman. I'm Bill Meeks...

II. - Episode summary/Main Discussion

 - Our rhyming, riddling episode summary

A. Host #1 Point[7]

    a. Host #1 Sub-Point

    b. Host #1 Sub-Point

B. Host #2 Point

    a. Host #2 Sub-Point

C. Host #1 Point

    a. Host #1 Sub-Point

D. Host #2 Point

    a. Host #2 Sub-Point

 - Look At This Joker

 - Featured Voicemail (Cast, Crew, or Listener)

 - Commercial Break/Patreon Read

---

[7] Find some way to visually identify everybody's points at a glance. With two co-hosts, I'd simply bold my points and leave Anne Marie's alone. If you have more than two co-hosts, or a special guest, I suggest using color coding. Make one person's points red, another's blue, etc.

E. Host #1 Point

    a. Host #1 Sub-Point

F. Host #2 Point

    a. Host #2 Sub-Point

G. Host #1 Point

    a. Host #1 Sub-Point

H. Host #2 Point

    a. Host #2 Sub-Point

Final Rating/Arbitrary Scale[8]

III. News/Speculation

    1. RATINGS[9]

    2. News Story #1

    3. News Story #2

    4. Discuss next episode's trailer

IV. Listener Feedback

---

[8] For the arbitrary scale, I'd usually come up with something during the podcast and type it in here. Even if you use a standard rating system, it's a good idea to add it to your doc so you can read it off and signal the main discussion is over.

[9] We always led our news segment with the ratings, an idea I stole from one of my favorite fancasts, Radio Free Skaro.

E-mail: legendsofgotham@gmail.com[10]

Twitter: @LegendsOfGotham

Facebook:

https://www.facebook.com/groups/LegendsOfGotham

Voicemail Number: (424) 274-2352

Voicemails

Letters

V. Show Close[11]

This outline worked for our podcast. Use it as a jumping-off point for your own Show Doc, or go in a completely different direction. Some people like mind-mapping software or index cards. The important thing is finding a way to organize your thoughts before you hit record or go live. It will keep your episode on-point, and your listeners will be able to tell you have a plan and that their ears are in safe hands.

---

[10] I suggest putting all your contact information in the doc so you can read it off without stumbling over or forgetting things.

[11] I always improvised this on the spot, but feel free to document what you want to say to wrap.

"If you have a guest, a good (show doc) will help them follow along because they will know what to expect." Rebecca Johnson, Host - Supergirl Radio

Now, where do you get all those points and sub-points to add to the doc? You're going to hate this word, but to get those points, you'll have to do your homework.

Doing Your Homework

> "If time allows, watch the episode at least twice. Once for enjoyment, the second for notes." - Derek O'Neill, TV Podcast Industries

Anything you review has dozens of threads to track: Characters, business names, plot points, references, and foreshadowing to name a few. Some viewers don't bother remembering all these threads, although many do. If you're a fancaster, tracking threads is part of the job description.

> "If I'm listening to a podcast, and the hosts are talking about anything, but it's obvious they do not know what they are talking about, I hit unsubscribe almost immediately." - Nathan Beatty, Host, **Creativity in Progress**

Every week, you take a test proctored by subject matter experts. You need to learn the material frontwards and backwards, just like when you were in school. You'll have to take notes, study, and bring it all together for the final exam.

You need to watch what you're reviewing more than once. As Derek O'Neil suggests in the quote above, twice is the bare minimum you should be watching things.

For your first watch, give it your full attention. No playing on your phone. Watch it as a fan. Ride the highs, brace for the lows, and enjoy the show. You love this, right? Put on your fan hat and geek out.

My actual notes for the Gotham episode "Smile Like You Mean It."

For your second watch, jot down anything that sticks out to you; Quotes, questions, favorite moments, thematic elements, and thoughts on the production design are all on the table. If you think it, write it down. As you go, scribble a star or other marker next to the points you're most excited about. Draw arrows to connect ideas. When you're done, go back through your notes and pick a number of topics you'd like to dig into, then add them as the main points in your Show Doc. I suggest listing the topics you're most passionate about first. For serialized shows and films, this means you might lead with the ending or cliffhanger. Next, comb through your notes for quotes, plot details, or impressions that match each topic and add them as sub-points.

> not end well for the Sirens...
> G. The Twinkie is Sick
> a. As I mentioned last week, I think we're getting more and more evidence that Lee Thompkins is infected with the Tetch virus.
> b. Her behavior this week is even more erratic. She injects a dude with truth serum amoung other out-of-character acts.
> c. I think the virus is starting to come out. Just like Mario and Barnes it's exposing a very powerful side of her that she's tried to keep hidden.
> d. She's always been kind and supportive, even when Jim is breaking the rules. She's fundamentally a good person, but I think a lot of that comes from her stopping herself with causing problems.
>   i. Now she's running into rooms to solve problems! She's letting her gut take the lead. Would the old Lee have tried to trick Jerome into killing himself? Never! But now she's okay

You'll note that my "Lee is totes infected" note from the notebook became a point titled "The Twinkie Is Sick" in the actual episode. You'll also note that I spell amoung like I'm from England.

Once you transfer your notes into the Show Doc, add an opening thesis statement, or tease, for each topic; something bold and clear. For example, there was an episode of Gotham which featured an entire community getting destroyed. My thesis statement for that topic was "Let's start at the end. Everybody in Haven is dead! But who did it?" This tells the listeners two important things right away:

1. The topic (Everybody in Haven is dead!)
2. What I thought was important about the topic (But who did it?)

Now, the listeners are leaning forward, and because I asked a question in my thesis, they think I have the answer, or at least a theory. **Make sure you have an answer, or at least a theory if you tease with a question.** If you don't deliver on a tease, you'll teach your listeners not to trust your teases.

Some fancasts post live threads on Twitter or Facebook as they watch an episode. It's a lot of fun, and a great opportunity to build relationships with your listeners. The downside is that you tend to miss a lot. It's hard to pay attention when you're making a snarky comment about an actor or searching for the perfect GIF to describe how a big reveal made you feel. If you live tweet, give it another "fan watch" before taking notes, since you're bound to miss key details as you jot things down.

If you have a co-host, be open to changing topics, or at least rearranging them. Sometimes you and your co-hosts will pick a similar topic. If you each have a different take, keep both, then put them together in the Show Doc for a natural long-form conversation. If you agree, one of you needs to volunteer to change your topic to add more variety to the discussion. Do it. Since your co-host is discussing the topic anyway, you'll still get to chime in.

Preparation is key to a successful fancast. By doing your homework, including reviewing your material multiple times, you'll commit key facts to your long-term memory using repetition. After I watched an episode twice for a podcast, I'd never watch it again, yet retain most of the important information. I don't have a great memory, but I still know most major and minor details from *Gotham* and *Once Upon A Time*, including the episode number and title those details appeared in. It's all because I took the time to watch the episodes twice when they came out.

Do your homework.

Keeping The Ball In The Air

"Be prepared. Things will go wrong, so try not to get overly hung up on your mistakes." - Derek O'Neill, TV Podcast Industries

In an ideal world, you'd have enough free time in a day to watch the show, prepare your Show Doc, record your podcast, then edit it down until it's absolutely perfect. In the real world, you won't always have time for that.

So, how do you ensure a high level of quality when you don't have time to edit? What if you live stream your podcast to Facebook or Twitch? To keep your podcast sounding professional, you just have to keep the ball in the air.

Picture a podcast as a ping pong game. One player serves— *PLOK*. The next player hits the ball back— *PLOK*. While the two players keep up that rhythm— *PLOK, PLOK, PLOK*— a simple game looks like a dance, each paddle swing as graceful as the Dance of the Little Swans. Then, a player misses the ball. The trance is broken. The ball bounces across the court— *PLOKLOP, PLOKLOP, PLOKLOP*. A player, probably you, runs awkwardly away from the table to retrieve it.

The entertainment value in a game of ping pong is the streak... How long can the players keep the ball in the air? As the minutes pass without a mistake— *PLOK, PLOK, PLOK*— the audience locks in to the players' rhythms, heads turning back and forth, until it's hard to tell where the performance ends and the audience begins. *PLOK, PLOK, PLOK.*

As a podcaster, you need to keep that ball in the air. Every time you miss your "swing," you break the rhythm you've established with your audience. Here are several common distractions that will make you miss the ball, along with several strategies that will make that little trot out to retrieve the ball a little less awkward.

Radical Agreement

The #1 way to keep the ball in the air is by maintaining your commitment to radical agreement. If you're maintaining your connection with your co-host, building off their offers, and avoiding the negative, you'll find yourself in a *PLOK, PLOK* rhythm you can maintain for hours at a time.

Mistakes

It's so easy to let a little mistake completely derail your show. Whether it's a forgotten fact or a curse word or getting halfway through your sentence before you realize you don't have a point, making mistakes always sucks. It's also easy to get flustered and frustrated, but you shouldn't hide those feelings from your listeners.

When you make a mistake, acknowledge it. Lean into it. Make it a running gag. Laugh it off. At the end of the day, you're only talking about a TV show or movie or whatever. If nobody got hurt, than the worst you've done is make yourself look silly. There's no shame in looking silly, especially for a podcaster.

Plan B

When you take the time to rewatch the episode, write notes, and prepare a Show Doc, you'll feel confident you can keep the ball in the air when you start your episode. On occasion, you'll find your topics weren't as rich as you thought, and you'll be left scrambling to fill the last ten minutes of your thirty minute show. This is why doing your homework is so important. If you keep your notes handy during your recording session, you'll have pages of potential discussion topics ready to go. Simply grab the notebook and flip around until you see something interesting. If you wrote something down, odds are you can vamp on it for a minute or three.

The Comments

Live streaming your podcast is a good idea. Instant feedback can only help you grow as a podcaster. As discussed in an earlier chapter, your engaged listeners are your greatest asset, and they'll be there for you any time you go live. That being said, it's important to balance serving these super fans with producing a quality show to attract new super fans.

It's easy to get lost in an ever-streaming comment feed, particularly when those comments call you out by name. If you look at the chat room or comments while you're in the middle of a thought, it's also easy to forget what your point was. This is another place where a co-host is invaluable. As you speak, your co-host can listen to what you're saying while keeping an eye on the comments and calling them out, when appropriate.

Don't look at comments when you're locked in a discussion. Scroll through them between topics to break things up, or use a bot to let listeners vote up comments to read and discuss.

Never scold your listeners for leaving a saying something distracting. You want interaction when you live stream your episode. If you scold somebody, they'll feel like they're hurting a podcast they love, and you might never hear from them again.

Co-host Etiquette

Sometimes, you'll fall out of sync with your co-host. Maybe one of you got distracted by the chat room, or maybe you were so busy thinking about your next point that you forgot to listen to theirs. However it happens, the best way to reconnect with your co-host is to ask them a question. A question shows your co-host you're still listening, and care about what they're saying.

Never interrupt your co-host, unless you're making a factual correction so your conversation doesn't go off-course based on bad facts. Always strive to build off whatever it is your co-host just said. You'll fall down off-topic "rabbit holes" on occasion. When you do, make sure your co-host finishes their thought before you transition back to the topic at hand.

If your co-host shuts you out and you can't seem to engage them, bring the topic back around to something you know they're passionate about. Mention a great moment from their favorite character, or reference a theory they came up with that turned out to be true. When your co-host shuts down, it's because you did something to sever your connection with them. Rebuild it as fast as you can.

Be Absurd

You can't always act absurd, but it will buy you time as you figure out how to fix a podcast recording gone bad. In moments of desperation and utter chaos, I would say outlandish things. Sometimes I'd make up parody lyrics for a song from *Frozen*. Maybe I'd show off my baby cry. One time I accused my co-host of murder. These tangents, and my co-host's reaction to them, always gave me more than enough time to refocus and figure out where we were going next. Most of the time, they were the best part of the show.

Suggesting you go off-script with absurdity might seem antithetical to what I've been preaching so far in this book, but no matter how much you plan, sometimes those plans will fail. If you're prepared to get a little absurd, a failed plan will never get in the way of keeping the ball in the air.

GIVING YOUR LISTENERS A VOICE

A s I discussed back in *The Café POV*, your listeners are your greatest asset, so you should always look for ways to get their voice on your podcast. People love discovering a new platform for their opinions. As a fancaster, you're positioned to offer a platform to diverse voices from all over the world. Giving your listeners a voice elevates your podcast in ways you won't expect. If you provide them with ample opportunities, their talent, insight, and sense of humor will surprise and delight you.

Your listeners offer a fresh perspective on your topic. Sometimes, they just look at things in a different way than you do. Oftentimes, you'll have subject matter experts in your audience for all kinds of topics. I had astrophysicists, fast food workers, psychologists, robotics scientists, librarians, and a bevy of other knowledgeable people in my audience who taught me about topics I'd never researched before. You'll also prove to the rest of your listeners that participating in the community is the best way to get on the podcast. Many of our listeners became fan-favorites, like Bobby Hawke.

"Bobby's Always Here"

Bobby Hawke called in with a *Once Upon A Time* theory as "Robert From Bradenton" a few months after we started the show in 2013. We loved Bobby's voicemails so much we gave him "pride of place" in our Feedback section. For the majority of the 500+ podcast episodes we produced, Bobby's voicemail was the first voicemail we played.

Bobby quickly became one of our most prolific contributors, there in the chat room for every live stream, sending in a voicemail ten minutes before we went live, and creating unique content we never asked for and always loved.

Bobby Hawke joins us for our panel at Tampa Bay Comicon in August 2016.

We got along with Bobby so well, we eventually handed him the reins to our first podcast, *Greetings From Storybrooke*, after we stepped away for reasons I'll discuss later. He even appeared with us at a live *Legends of Gotham* panel in Tampa Bay, near Bradenton. Bobby was always there with support and encouragement. His presence made our podcasts better. When we'd set up to go live, we'd invariably open the chat room and have this exchange:

> Bill: Well, Bobby's here.
>
> Anne Marie: Bobby's always here.

Bobby | I definitely got a Buffy vibe recently

Bobby chatting during a "Greetings From Storybrooke"
live stream.

Bobby's always here, and I hope he always will be. I
don't get to talk to Bobby as often as I'd like these days,
but we're still tight. Our kids have met. I know that,
whenever I'm hatching my next creative project, I can
always depend on Bobby to participate, or at least cheer
me on. I can count on Bobby Hawke.

> "There's no end to the different ways it's fun to
> connect with people on the internet. All you gotta
> do is put in the effort, and there is this great
> reward." Justin Robert Young, Host - Who's The
> Boss?

We had a lot of "Bobbys": Hope Mullinax and Wynn
Mercere and Dawn Owar and Other Annemarie and
Debbie Deb Deb Deb and Dave from Michigan and
Michael Lucero and Angel and Tony and Monica and
Amy P. and Bud Vanderkay and Josh Phelps and Liz and

Woo and Nicole and Niko and Lady Jae and Peter Price and so many others whose names escape me at the moment. These people felt like friends because these people *are* my friends. By having them appear on our podcasts, we started a two-way conversation that's still ongoing, long after we quit fancasting.

"Magic Juice" by Nicole Troyer, mailed to us to celebrate the 100th episode of Greetings From Storybrooke.

Sure, monetizing your podcast is important. You should want good numbers, as you define them. Using your podcast to refine your craft is great too. But my greatest accomplishment in podcasting was the community we built, the "Bobbys" who all banded together to cheer us on as we stumbled and fumbled our way through getting good. I'm glad we were able to give these people's whacked-out theories and brilliant insights a platform. We also had the privilege of introducing these people to each other. Some of our community members have teamed up on their own projects, or meet up at conventions, or chat back and forth on Twitter about whatever they're obsessed with now. Whenever I see these echos of our community as I mindlessly scroll on my phone, it makes all the time and energy we put into these podcasts feel like it was worth it.

I hope your podcast finds a Bobby.

Using Listeners As Guests

Finding Your Bobbys

It isn't hard to find your Bobbys. You might have listeners whose names you know, the ones who banter with you in the chat during your stream or call in with a voicemail every week. Start by reaching out to these people, if you have them. Do it on a personal basis, either through e-mail or a direct message, so your other listeners don't accuse you of playing favorites.

You kind of are, though.

> "In my experience with large and small audiences, 80% will never tell you anything. That doesn't mean they don't love you! It's just podcast feedback is not on their to-do list. I stumble across listeners that are like 'Oh, Kevin. Love the show. Never call in, never send an e-mail, but keep doing it.'" Kevin Bachelder, Host - Tuning Into SciFi TV

If you don't know any Bobbys, don't get discouraged. Consider how many pieces of content you consume in a year, podcasts included. Let's say it's 300 pieces of content. How many of those creators did you interact with online? 1? 10? 25? Whatever your number, it's a tiny percentage, and you loved a lot of the other content just as much, if not more, than the content you interacted with online. You have a lot of listeners in the shadows, drinking up your content. Why not shine a flashlight and see who's out there?

> "Try to find the easiest way that your audience can communicate with you. Pay attention to where anybody is interacting with you, go there, and ask direct questions." Justin Robert Young, Host - Who's The Boss?

Book guests by asking for volunteers on your podcast at the top of your Listener Feedback segment, since the same people who enjoy sending in feedback would love to give you their feedback live. Offer a link to a form they can fill in. Ask for their availability and audio set-up. Sites like Google Forms put the responses into a spreadsheet you can work from when you need to schedule a guest. When we did a spin-off podcast about *Once Upon A Time In Wonderland*, we decided to have a new listener join us every week. We asked for volunteers to fill out the form at the end of episodes of *Greetings From Storybrooke*, then I'd work from the spreadsheet to schedule guests for *Greetings From Wonderland*, striking out names as we had people on.

Our first live stream, a "Once Upon A Time In Wonderland" wrap-up discussion.

Put out the call on social media, but be warned that some of the people responding might not even listen to your podcast. A lot of fans follow anything, including fancasts, related to a property they love as a matter of course, and might not pay attention to your actual podcast. If one of these people responds, you can still invite them on as a guest. Worst case scenario, you'll keep the ball in the air through an awkward interview. In the best case scenario, you'll convert your guest into a regular listener. You'll also hear a fresh perspective from somebody outside your community.

Managing Guests

When you have a listener on as a guest, all my points about radical agreement with your co-host still apply. In fact, it's even more important to have a "yes, and" attitude with a guest, particularly one who is already a big fan of your podcast. Remember, your guest is a stand-in for every listener, since every listener will imagine what they would do if they were on your podcast. If you don't get along, your listeners might take it personally, and they'll stop contributing to your podcast. After all, if you could hang up on "Bobby," you might hang up on them.

On the technical side, always do a test call with your guest to make sure their set up will work for your show. At the bare minimum, you need to be able to hear them without a ton of background noise. If you can, record the listener's audio on a separate track from your audio, so you can clean it up in the editing process. You should also consider making a backup recording, which we'll cover more in the chapter on *Engaging The Cast And Crew*.

Sometimes, due to no fault of their own, a beloved community member will be a dud of a guest. Sometimes they'll even get confrontational. Apply the *Café POV* philosophy, and the skills I taught you about keeping the ball in the air, to make sure you come out the other side with a podcast that still entertains your listeners.

Remember, this is your show, and sometimes you might have to make a hard decision to save it. We never had an invited guest cause a scene, but we've had issues opening up Skype to take calls on the live stream. We've had trolls threaten other people in the chat, use derogatory terms, and personally insult the hosts.

I believe most trolls are fans who haven't realized that they're fans yet, and you'll learn ways to convert them into your most devoted listeners in the next chapter. On occasion, you'll have to make a hard choice and pull the plug on a guest. When you do, apologize to your listeners, then explain why you did it in plain terms, even if the reason seems obvious. The few times I've booted a caller, I felt just awful about it, but there's degrees between providing a platform for listeners and letting them burn it to the ground. If you're transparent when explaining your side to your listeners, they'll understand and support you. Try to sweep it under the rug, and you risk fracturing the community you've spent so much time building.

Inventing New Ways To Get Listeners Involved

You can involve listeners in your show without having them as a guest on a normal episode. Season-based episodic television in particular gives you plenty of breaks in your schedule to publish experimental content and get your listeners involved. The opportunities available to you rely on your podcast's format, but I have a few ideas that helped us keep the community (and the podcast) going in the off-season.

Season Break Hangouts

We got in the habit of inviting listeners, as well as other podcasters in our niche, on before and after every season. We'd also do it during a show's winter break to discuss the half-season. We used Google Hangouts on Air via YouTube to stream these Hangouts live to our YouTube channel, which has a lot of great features for streaming podcasts like automatic audio normalizing and scene switching. Hangouts are easy for most people to set up, and your guests can join via their phone or computer. The quality is "just okay," but it's consistently "just okay." You might notice some drops and buffering while you're recording, but you usually won't see them in the final video.

"Teaming up with other podcasts is a great way to fill that 'dead space' and build the community around your show." Darrell Darnell, Co-Founder - Golden Spiral Media

LEGENDS OF GOTHAM #20
Podcaster Roundtable #2

Our second Podcaster Roundtable for Legends of Gotham, streamed the week before Gotham came back after winter break.

"We've always been friends with other (Firefly podcasts). We're all just one big community. Some will be more content-based, some will be more news-based. But we all get along." Les Howard, Host - The Signal

Limit your guest list to no more than four people other than you and your co-hosts. The more people on your live stream, the less likely you'll be able to keep everybody focused on the topic at hand. It's easy for the conversation to go off on wild tangents that will make everybody feel lost. To guard against this, prep your guests ahead of time with a simple system to keep everybody on-task and organized. Be the ringleader. For the most part, your guests will sit back and let you run the show, calling on them and leading the conversation. Most teleconferencing tools have a private chat feature. Suggest your guests "raise their hand" in the chat so you know to call on them.

For the actual discussion, we'd break the Show Doc out into categories like Favorite Moment, Favorite Character, and Biggest Unanswered Question. We'd also discuss key moments in the season (or the season so far). Since you'll have more voices, you don't need to do as much prep work for panel discussions. People have been listening to what you and your co-hosts think about the show all season. Just sit back, make sure the chaos remains somewhat organized, and let your guests shine.

"My co-host, Morgan, is quick on her feet and hilariously witty, so when her comments on the bizarre fashion choices Lena Luthor made us laugh, we turned that into a segment called 'Lena Luthor: Boardroom or Ballroom,' where we lovingly analyze the outfits that Lena Luthor has worn. I recognize that this aspect of the podcast is Morgan's idea and that listeners have embraced it because of Morgan's sense of humor, so I don't mind taking a backseat. Listeners love it so much that they request it before we even have a chance to record!"
Rebecca Johnson, Host - Supergirl Radio

Hypothetical Fan Fiction

One year, *Once Upon A Time* had a particularly long winter break. We'd just started live streaming our podcasts a few months earlier, and were worried about taking a couple months off and losing people. Hope Mullinax, one of our most engaged listeners, suggested a fun idea: What if we did a series of specials where we examined key moments in *Once's* mythology, and considered how the show would have gone if those moments had played out differently?

Our first Once If...? special, inspired by Hope's suggestion.

We called the series *Once If...?*, and it produced some of the most fun, electric, and creative interactions we ever had on the show. This format let everybody show off their strengths, including their encyclopedic knowledge of *Once* and their hot takes on where the show had gone wrong. Discussions often got heated, with many firmly-held opinions butting up against one another, but since everybody knew each other from the chat room, and it was all hypothetical anyway, we all walked away laughing.

Rally The Troops

When inspiration strikes, make a specific request for feedback from your listeners. The first time we did this, we started a 'shipping war' on *Greetings From Storybrooke.*

During the course of one podcast, it came out that I loved the relationship between Emma Swan and Captain Hook, while Anne Marie preferred Emma's relationship with Rumpelstiltskin's son Baelfire. I knew, from browsing online forums and social media, that this was a key disagreement between fans of *Once*. We leaned into it, asking listeners to weigh in on social media using the hashtags #TeamBill and #TeamAnneMarie.

Kathy
@kathygribble

Replying to @GFStorybrooke

@GFStorybrooke #teamannemarie 4 life!

10:44 PM · Mar 22, 2015 · Twitter for Android

One of many tweets in support of #TeamAnneMarie.

Our listeners responded in kind, allowing us to devote a big part of our next Feedback episode to the brewing "controversy." It was a safe way for our viewers to vent their 'shipping frustrations, and became a running joke our listeners brought back often through the years. Near the end, we'd still get e-mails signed #TeamAnneMarie. Never #TeamBill.

Related Media Reviews

Rebecca Johnson and @HolyBatPastor join us to discuss Batman v Superman: Dawn of Justice.

Include listeners when you discuss media tangentially related to the content you cover. When we reviewed *Batman v Superman* on *Legends of Gotham*, for example, I knew we had to get *Supergirl Radio* host Rebecca Johnson and Batman bat fan Holy Bat Pastor from our chat room to join in on the proceedings. We all liked the film, but don't hold that against us too much, or else we'll say your mom's name at just the right moment and blow your Bat-mind.

If you find people you work well with, consider bringing them back on a semi-regular basis. If you find yourself without a co-host, you'll have somebody ready to jump in and help you out.

Expert Interviews

As you get to know your listeners, you'll learn more about their particular passions. Sometimes, you'll discover synergy between their expertise and the content you're covering. If the creators announce their upcoming season will be inspired by the classic story *Beowolf*, bring that English Lit professor who wrote you a few months back on to discuss the original story, and how it might fit into the upcoming season. Maybe you have a *Mr. Robot* podcast, and somebody in your chat room specializes in dissociative identity disorder, hacking, or black hoodies. Have them on to talk about the show from an insider's perspective.

"A listener wrote in with a comment on Kara Zor-El's status as a refugee, something the Supergirl show itself asserts in its opening narration. (We) put it out to the listeners that if any of them had thoughts on whether it was the correct use of the term 'refugee.' A few days later, we received two different emails from listeners who had 20 and 30 years in law, respectively, some of which involved constitutional law and working in Washington, D.C. Because their feedback was so scholarly and amazing, we invited both of these loyal listeners/legal experts onto the podcast for a special episode on Kara Zor-El's refugee status. And now, anytime we have a legal question brought up by a storytelling choice, we get our 'Supergirl Radio Legal Consultants' on the case." Rebecca Johnson, Host - Supergirl Radio

If none of these ideas fit your podcast, come up with some that do, or let your listeners do it for you. Like I said, the *Once If...?* idea wasn't ours. Hope came up with it, then we made it happen for her. If your community isn't volunteering suggestions, ask them. I guarantee you there are listeners out there just waiting for you to give them a voice on your podcast.

FEED THE TROLLS

I believe in the power, intelligence, and experience of other people. Because I believe in other people, I assume that they're acting in good faith, with mutual respect. This bites me in the butt as often as it helps me, but it's one of those core beliefs I just can't shake. This translated to me letting pretty much anybody say pretty much anything they wanted. For the most part, our listeners treated that open invitation with respect. I didn't even read their e-mails or listen to their voicemails before we broadcast them live on the stream, so complete was my trust in our storytellers.

Yes, some listeners betrayed that trust, but not as many as you'd think. I'm sure I don't remember a lot of our worst trolls, but that's because we converted them into fans of the show. It's not hard, and trolls-turned-fans are some of the most supportive listeners you'll have. Imagine all that negative energy they've wasted trolling over the years converted into positive energy and directed towards your show. If you can get them on your side, and they often already are on your side, you'll have powerful allies spreading the word about your podcast and contributing to your community in positive, if seemingly bizarre, ways.

Who Trolls (Usually) Are

Having been a netizen[12] since the 1990s, I've run into a lot of trolls. Sometimes they came after me. Other times I'd watch them devour something I loved from a safe distance. While every person is different, I've found a few common traits in online trolls that allowed me to empathize with them, and taught me how to either convert them or bore them, until they were no longer a drain on our community.

Don't assume every troll you run into fits this profile. There are aggressive, nasty, dangerous people out there, and you need to keep your wits about you, especially when you're putting so much of yourself into your podcast. But, if you take a moment to understand why people troll, you'll be able to deal with them in a productive way and take back control of your show.

> "Since the internet is anonymous, sometimes people think they can say anything they wish without repercussions, so they do. They can't see the person they may be hurting, so they don't care. Trolling adds tension to the community, and may scare away new visitors who assume that sort of behavior is either the norm, or tolerated within the group." - Noel in Savannah, GA

In the above response from a trolling survey I conducted back in 2007, Noel nails the biggest reason

---

12 That's a citizen of the internet for you Zoomers.

people troll. We're social creatures who have been conditioned over thousands of years to care about how other human beings react to our behavior. When somebody reacts negatively to something we do in real life, it triggers a fight or flight response and teaches us that, at least in the current context, our behavior is unacceptable. When somebody types out a heated response on Facebook, it doesn't set off the same alarm bells in a troll's head as an in-person confrontation. No voice shouts at him to back off or let up. So, he keeps pushing that button until he gets a response, the bigger the better.

Trolls want a response because, for whatever reason, they feel unheard. They might feel unheard in their real life, in their online life, or both. Everybody wants to be heard. Not having a voice can make you feel powerless. After all, if nobody is listening to you, do you really even exist?

Other people might troll you because they enjoy your podcast and want to be a part of your community, but are too afraid to try. They'll project their frustrations towards you, as well as their fellow listeners. Some trolls might listen to your podcast so much they've developed an entire back-and-forth relationship with you in their heads, then they'll resent you for not maintaining that relationship, even though they never said one word to you before they started trolling. It doesn't seem very fair, does it? To be judged for a relationship you didn't even realize you were in? It might not be your fault, but a troll will make it your problem.

Sometimes, but only sometimes, trolls are just assholes with nothing better to do than to make your life difficult. These are the hopeless cases that will back you into a corner and force you to act. I hope you never encounter one of these trolls, but if you broadcast on the internet, it's going to happen.

We had our own issues with one of the assholes, involving stalking and physical attacks in real life and personal threats over the course of two years. I won't go into details here, since I've talked about it plenty with my loved ones and therapist. Before all that happened, I'd formed the core belief about trolls I've outlined above, that everybody deserves a chance, and it's worth the time to help somebody find their voice. After our troll put me through the ringer, it hardened my resolve. If I let an asshole's actions against me and my family rob me of my belief in the power of other people, to me that would be letting her win.

Dealing With Trolls

The common wisdom is that you shouldn't "feed the trolls," which basically means you should ignore them. This approach can work, but for many trolls it simply emboldens them to become more and more disruptive until you're forced to respond.

Screw that. If your troll wants attention, then by all means give it to them, but do it on your terms. You can't control a troll, but you can control your reaction. If a troll doesn't get the response they crave, they'll eventually apologize or give up.

The Reverse Troll

This is the best way to vanquish a troll, because you do it with a smile. Nothing is more frustrating to trolls than a happy victim. When encountering a new troll, the Reverse Troll is almost always my first move.

Listen to what your troll has to say, then respond to it earnestly, honestly, and with a healthy sense of humor. Remember radical agreement? You can weaponize it. If they ask why you're so ugly, go into a monologue about how your parent's genes didn't quite fit together right. If they find your voice annoying, agree, then spend a few minutes making your voice deeper and sexier than it already is. However they try to get under your skin, radically agree, then use your wit to add your own punchline to their joke. This works best if you don't acknowledge it's a trick. The more you can sell it as an honest reaction from the friendliest version of your podcast persona, the more you'll "troll the troll." Do it well, and your troll won't be a troll for long. Your listeners will also find it hilarious.

The Socratic Method

There was this bro named Socrates back in the day. He was pretty chill. He spent most of his days hanging out with his friends, drinking ancient wine, and talking about what it means to be alive. Basically, he was like your northeastern Liberal Arts college roommate. He probably smoked just as much pot. He was a respected teacher, but he didn't talk *at* his students. He preferred to talk *with* them, then he'd let their curiosity guide his teachings. He didn't shout his opinions at his students. He asked them questions which helped them come up with the right answers on their own.

Using the Socratic Method on trolls is super effective because it forces the troll to question their actions, opinions, and methods. Instead of telling them how their trolling makes you feel, ask them questions that show them how frustrating they really are.

I'll give you an example. Imagine LeETHaX0r69-420 enters your chat room, and says all the other people in the chat room are "lame AF[13]." Here's what using the Socratic approach looks like in action.

LeETHaX0r69-420: All you dumbasses are lame AF

HOST: Lame? Why do you think we're lame?

LeETHaX0r69-420: nobody knows wtf they are talking about

HOST: Oh no! What did we get wrong?

LeETHaX0r69-420: That bald guy on the stream said Detective Wallace didn't know about the icepick killer like a dumbass!

HOST: The bald guy? Me?

LeETHaX0r69-420: Yeah.

HOST: Well, I'm not quite bald yet, but I thought for sure Wallace had never heard about the icepick killer. When did that happen?

LeETHaX0r69-420: The Christmas episode, duh. You know, the chief guy told him right before they made out in that closet.

HOST: Oh, yeah! Sorry I forgot about that pivotal scene. Thanks for the correction. Was there anything else we got wrong?

LeETHaX0r69-420: nah, bro. its chill.

---

[13] "Lame as f—"

By thinking through your responses, keeping them positive, and consistently hitting the ping pong ball back in the troll's direction, you'll keep him on the defensive, distracting him from his trollish ways until he accidentally has a thoughtful exchange like the one above. That example is a best-case scenario, but I've questioned many trolls into submission. Sometimes, it just takes the right question.

Trolls Make Great Fans

I've always said a troll is just a fan who isn't ready to admit they're a fan. In fact, I've said it several times in this book... Maybe even in this chapter! It's true. If you encounter a troll, judo his negativity away, and he changes his behavior and sticks around, you've uncovered a fan in hiding. Give him what he came for: Attention.

Whenever I'd see the name of a former troll in our chat room, I'd call them out on the stream and thank them for showing up, often right at the top of the show. When it came time to ask for feedback, I'd call them out and ask them to leave more voicemails. If a troll sticks around, it's because they've earned your respect, or you've earned theirs. Either way, they'll be one of your most devoted community members because you fought for them, and won.

When Enough Is Enough

Sad fact, some trolls don't want to change. They like who they become when they get online, and there's nothing you can do to change it. Everybody has a line. Some fancasts draw the line at language. Any reasonable podcaster would agree that racism, sexism, or xenophobia are deal-breakers. Eventually, they'll push you past your line, and you'll need to take action.

Wherever your line is, make sure your listeners know about it, and be prepared to explain it every time somebody crosses it and you have to take action. This is discipline on a public stage, so make sure the rules are clear and the punishment is fair. Sure, it's your show, but nobody likes a dictator. If you encourage listeners to freely express themselves like I did, a lack of clarity will discourage them from contributing to your show.

I usually give trolls four chances. My co-host Anne Marie always said I was too forgiving, but I like walking away from a conflict knowing I did everything I could to resolve it. Sometimes these chances would play out over several weeks of voicemails. Other times, they would occupy thirty seconds of a live stream. Depends on the troll and how they troll you.

- 1st Offense - The first offense is when you'll want to try out my techniques like the Reverse Troll. This is the best time to stop a troll, before they throw a wrench into your podcast.

- 2nd Offense - If my techniques don't help, tell the troll what they did wrong, then let them know that if they don't stop, you'll have to take action.
- 3rd Offense - Mute them. Most chat platforms have a feature which mutes or freezes a user in your chat room or comments section. Think of it as a temporary ban, where the user's comments are hidden from view for a set period of time, or until you decide to let them speak again. If your troll uses voicemail or e-mail, don't run their feedback. It's up to you how long, and if, you ever give them their voice back. If they reach out and seem apologetic, consider giving them one more shot. Set firm rules, and let them know breaking those rules will result in a permanent ban. If they don't reach out, consider going in quietly a week or two later to unmute their account. Most trolls will move on, and if they act up again you can ban them. However, if they're ready to be a member of the community, shout them out when you see them and be thankful they've changed their ways.
- 4th Offense - Banish your troll with a full, permanent ban. If this person continues to attack your podcast and your community after so many chances, odds are they'll never stop. At this point, you'll have no other option than to block them forever on as many platforms as you can. Set up

an e-mail filter, if needed. It's hard to host a podcast when you're dealing with drama, so if you can't convert the drama into something positive, cut your losses and get on with the show.

It's important to give a troll a chance to redeem herself, but some people are trouble from the start, and you should shut them down as soon as possible. If anybody ever threatens violence, or makes an inappropriate comment about you, your co-hosts, or your guests, don't be afraid to slap them with the ban hammer straight away. When we moved our live streams to Twitch we had to insta-ban people a few times, but I don't feel bad about it. They were jerks, and they had no interest in our show anyway.

The safety and emotional wellbeing of you and your community is more important than my lofty ideals of free expression. Guidelines are great, but when you find yourself needing to act decisively to protect everything you've built hosting a podcast about Micronauts or whatever, don't hesitate.

ENGAGING THE CAST & CREW

N othing gives you more credibility than engaging the cast and crew of the production you're reviewing. It's an official Seal of Approval for your podcast, and a reputation builder within the community. It also adds value for your listeners, especially if you pass on their questions during an interview.

You might be gun-shy about contacting your favorite actor or showrunner. Don't be. You're offering them a direct line to their most passionate fans, ones passionate enough to listen to an hour-long podcast.

Most creators welcome the chance to discuss their work, provided they have the time. A retweet or follow from a celebrity account can also net you new followers, some of whom will eventually listen to your show. Who knows? You might even spark up a friendship over drinks with a creator after a convention panel.

When you land an exclusive interview, you'll have a great reason to promote your podcast wherever fans are hanging out online, particularly if you get a big scoop. Your interview subject will also spread the word, adding even more credibility to your burgeoning podcast.

You don't get anything you don't ask for. As long as you're respectful of the person's time, and act professionally throughout the process, you have nothing to lose by asking. The worst that can happen is they'll say no, or you won't get a response. Better to try and fail, then to assume your show is too small and never know if they would have said yes.

Social Media

Thanks to enhanced filter settings for "Verified" users, social media channels aren't as effective at reaching celebrities as they were even a few years ago. Still, actors are encouraged to live tweet during an episode or host a Q&A on Facebook Live after it airs, so there are times when they'll be paying attention to their feed.

As discussed in an earlier chapter, you should start your podcast months before the show premieres. This includes creating social accounts for your show. Starting early will give you a chance to build up followers by posting updates about the show as news and official promotional material leaks. With any luck, and proper tagging, this will catch the eye of the show's social media team and get you on a follow list.

Jada Pinkett Smith ✅
@jadapsmith Follows you
🔗 redtabletalk.com 📅 Joined June 2009
204 Following **1.4M** Followers

We just call her Jada.

What's a follow list? It's a list handed out by the marketing team to key cast and crew, as well as new actors who join the show after launch. We were on *Gotham's* follow list, which meant we got follows from big names like Jada Pinkett-Smith and Ben McKenzie. The follow list also gave us an early warning for upcoming guest stars, since they'd follow our Twitter account a week or two before the casting was announced.

The follow list will open you up to swag you can offer to your listeners as giveaways. If you get offered a freebie, make sure you mention the product on your show. A lot. If you don't, the offers will dry up.

Our "Gotham Sweetheart Giveaway" commercial.

Leverage free SWAG to grow your show. When Diamond Select Toys sent us a couple dozen *Gotham* action figures, we did a fake commercial that promoted the toys, the contest, and our podcast. We played the promo in every podcast we did for about a month, and cross-posted it to our Facebook page, YouTube channel, and other social sites like Reddit. We had a few goals for our podcast at the time: More Apple Podcast reviews, more Patreon patrons, and more Twitch subscribers. Three ways to enter, two of them free. In the end, we reached our goals, and gave our listeners fun prizes while we did it. We even got to keep the action figures and set pieces from the commercial to use as props on the live stream.

Getting followed by official accounts will help you break through the noise of social media and contact talent directly. Be careful with this. If you're too forward, or too demanding, it might get you unfollowed and blocked by the cast member you're contacting, which could lead to you getting kicked off the follow list.

If you aren't on the follow list, that doesn't mean you can't engage with the cast and crew. Tweet them funny GIFs that reference something that happened to their character on the show, or chip in when they ask fans for donations to their favorite charity. Bigger stars might not manage their own accounts, but their social media team will still inform them about significant interactions. They'll also let them know if you're pouring Haterade, so don't tag them if you have something critical to say about them or their performance. It's just rude, and it isn't going to help your podcast.

Their "People"

"Have your people call my people." - Various Hollywood Big Shots

Hollywood people, especially actors, have "people." Agents and managers and publicists and business managers and personal assistants. These people help protect them from things that will distract these professionals from their ultimate goals: Performing, then booking their next gig.

You probably don't have "people." That's okay. Many in the media are starting to see the power of podcasting. Sure, you'll have to compete with the likes of Conan O'Brien, the happy lady from *Nailed It*, and Pauly Shore. Some celebrities have special agents who handle their podcast bookings. Remember, you're offering these celebrities a direct channel to a curated group of their super fans. That's a powerful thing, one that extends far beyond their current project.

"The CW cracks down on their writers from making appearances on any web shows to discuss the episodes that they write. We've been told that explicitly. Showrunners, maybe, but not individual writers of episodes. That's why we have tried to reach outside of the writing staff. We've tried to build a relationship with the Supergirl prop guy. We've invited actors like the chick who played Kelly in Season 1. She was a bit character who became beloved on Supergirl Radio and it was a nice get for us. So even if you don't have access to the head honchos, there are lots of other people involved in the show you might be able to talk to." Rebecca Johnson, Host - Supergirl Radio

On the other hand, their people might consider your podcast one of those *distractions* they're supposed to protect their clients from. If so, you'll get an automated rejection, or you'll just never hear back. Again, you have nothing to lose by asking, as long as you're polite, professional, and respectful of their time.

Finding Out Who To Contact

First, figure out who you need to contact. Luckily, we live in the information age, and there are several resources online that will help you.

Google

A publicist or agent might be a simple Google search away. Type the actor or crew member's name in quotes, then add a plus sign and try keywords like "management" or "publicist."

A sample search for Tom Cruise's publicist, which surprisingly gave me a name.

Agents, publicists, and managers love bragging about their clients. If it's a smaller agency, they might have the person you're trying to interview listed on their website, right next to the agent's contact information. Now, you aren't going to reach Tom Cruise's people using this method. Even his people have people. But, if you're angling for a supporting character, or even a fresh-faced lead without much of a following, this method might work for you.

The actor's official website, if they have one, might have contact details for their management team. Many official sites have a contact form, but these are usually the digital equivalent of writing a message to your landlocked grandma in Idaho, then stuffing it in a bottle and tossing it into the Pacific Ocean.

If you don't see anything in the first page of search results, dig deeper. You could find a name in an article from an entertainment trade magazine, or discover the actor mentioned their publicist in an interview on Access Hollywood.

IMDBPro

If you don't turn anything up on Google, there's a ninety-nine percent chance you'll find something on IMDBPro, the industry-facing side of Amazon's Internet Movie Database.

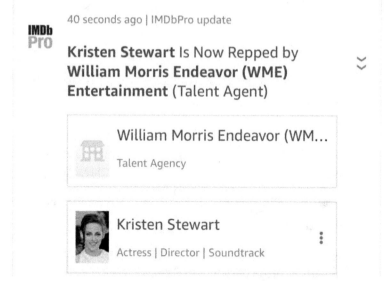

For your Twilight fancast.

Nearly everybody has contact information on here, since IMDB is an essential tool used throughout the entertainment industry for casting and hiring crew. I used to work at an agency in Los Angeles, and most of the employees had IMDBPro up at all times.

The bad news? IMDBPro is a paid service. As of this writing, it cost $19.99 per month, or $149.99 per year. That's not outrageous, but if you aren't making money off your podcast, it's probably not worth it. Luckily, IMDBPro offers a 30-Day free trial on their homepage, which is more than enough time for you to look up contact information for everybody from the lead actress to that extra with the weird hair.

Social Media

As a last resort, or a first resort if you're feeling lazy, contact people directly over social media. Tweet them on Twitter, message their Facebook fan page, or DM them on Instagram. This probably won't help you with bigger names if they don't follow you already, but I've had a high response rate. Building a relationship with a celebrity on social, by interacting with their posts and mentioning them in your own posts, is a great way to pole vault over those pesky people protecting the person you're trying to book on your podcast.

If you give social media a shot, keep it simple. Give them your voicemail number and ask a specific question. Hollywood people are busy, but some are willing to make a quick phone call. If they do, there probably won't be any back-and-forth, which is why you want to provide your question up front. If you use a service like Google Voice for your show's voicemail, make sure to check your Spam folder. To protect themselves, many celebrities will block their number from Caller ID, which often sends the message to Spam.

If this goes well, you have an open door to approach them for a full interview down the road.

Studio/Network Contacts

"Make sure you contact the press office of the channel or service that will air the show. They sometimes organize interviews with the cast." - Derek O'Neill, TV Podcast Industries

It doesn't hurt to reach out to the press offices of the network or studio. Keep the request general. Ask if you can speak to a creator or cast member, but don't be too picky. The lead actress is probably booked up, but you might land an interview with the guy who plays her dad.

To find studio/network contacts, use the same methods I discussed earlier. Just replace the actor's name with a studio or network name, and look for "Public Relations" or "Promotions" staff. Some network and studio sites have a company directory with a breakdown of who to contact for a specific show or movie. If there are multiple names listed for your show, consider CC'ing everybody. You never know who actually reads their e-mail.

Reaching Out

> "We tried to reach out to the studio for interviews, but they don't want people doing interviews when the show's not on. Meanwhile, we're trying to keep the fans engaged while the show's on hiatus, so we have different agendas."
> Darrell Darnell, Co-Founder - Golden Spiral Media

Once you identify your person's people, it's important to keep your message short and informative.

For example, this is a censored version of an e-mail I sent to engage a key creator from one of the shows I used to review, after first making contact with them and their publicist on Twitter.

*Dear **REDACTED**,*

Thanks for the Twitter chat earlier today.

*My name is Bill Meeks. I'm the person behind the **REDACTED** Twitter account, and a co-host on the podcast, **REDACTED**, which reaches around 15,000 **REDACTED** fans every episode.*

*We loved Season 1 of **REDACTED**, and were hoping we could chat with **REDACTED** for 15-20 minutes about what's coming up in Season 2. Our listeners would love some teases. If we have time, we'd also like to ask a few questions about Season 1. We want this to be a friendly interview by fans, for fans. We'll pre-*

tape, and we'd be happy to edit around any potential spoilers that come up before we share the interview with our listeners.

*Can we schedule some time with **REDACTED** this coming Thursday? If there is a better day, please let us know. We'd like to have the interview in-hand and edited before our recording next Tuesday.*

*Thanks, **REDACTED**. Can't wait to chat with **REDACTED**!*

Bill Meeks

This reads like your basic friendly e-mail, but there's an intentional structure to it.

- **Establish who you are and why they should keep reading** — Introduce yourself by name, and let them know of any meaningful interactions you've had with them or their client.
- **Establish your credibility** — Prove that you aren't a distraction. It might feel braggy, but this is the time to brag. If you want them to take you seriously, you need to let them know who they'll reach through your podcast. If your show has less than 15,000 downloads, don't worry! No matter what your numbers are, remember that your

audience is filled with passionate fans, exactly the kinds of people your interviewee and their people want to connect with.

- **The "ask"** — Let them know what you want to talk about, how long you think it will take, and give them an assurance that you'll allow them to have input on the final interview before you release it. That might go afield of journalistic ethics, but I don't consider fancasting journalism. Podcasting has gained more acceptance over the years, but companies and creators are more nervous than ever about losing control of their message. If you want to talk about a challenging topic, let them know up front. Don't ask a "gotcha" question out of nowhere, and if you do, be prepared for it to be your last interview with somebody from that particular production.

- **Action item** - Close out your request with next steps. If it's an interview, schedule it. If it's a Q&A, send them a link to the questions and include your deadline. Let them know what they need to do next. Keep it simple.

- **Express enthusiasm** — Close by letting them know you're excited and appreciative for the opportunity to talk to somebody who works on one of your favorite things. As a fancaster, you won't have to fake your enthusiasm!

This structure works on a phone call too. Feel free to steal it, then jot down some notes to work from before you dial the agency's number.

Conventions

> "We got a press pass for a big convention that had a lot of cast members there. We asked questions about the show and clearly told them where we're from. That got us a big interview." - Derek O'Neill, TV Podcast Industries

Conventions can be tricky. Many conventions have free or discounted admission for podcasters who contribute to the convention, either by offering press coverage or as a panelist, but there is a hidden cost. In order to get the big names, conventions write long lists of rules you need to follow. These rules limit how you will approach celebrities, and if you can ask them for an interview on your podcast.

Appearing as a panelist at Dragon Con 2013, along with fellow fancasters Rebecca Johnson and Hope Mullinax.

In my time as a fancaster, and as a convention reporter for the website Bleeding Cool, I've seen the full spread.

Sometimes, you're allowed to talk to the actors, but you can't mention your podcast. Other times, it's a laid back affair and you can ask people for a quick interview at their table in the Walk of Fame.

Our first live "Greetings From Storybrooke" panel at Regal Con 2015 in Anaheim, CA. (Pictured: Guests Becca Canote and Jeff Roney)

Whatever the rules, if you want access, you need to know and follow them. I've bent the rules before, and it nearly got me kicked out of the event. To be fair, the actress I was talking to asked me why I was at the convention, and the podcast was the reason why, but I'd agreed to the rules beforehand and bending them almost cost me my access before the convention even started.

If you aren't attending the convention in an official capacity, get a little bolder. Attend a panel, identify yourself as a fancaster before asking your question, then swing by the celebrity's table and thank them for answering your question. If they aren't busy, strike up a conversation about the show, or another project they've worked on that you've enjoyed. In anything, you'll get a lot farther by establishing a real relationship before making your "ask." I mean, don't be a stalker or anything, but have an actual conversation with them. If the actor seems uncomfortable, or starts to look around for their agent or a handler, thank them for their time and disengage. If you come on too strong, you could still land in hot water with the convention staff.

Getting a press badge is the best way to go, since you can schedule interviews through the press office. Request press credentials by visiting the convention's website. You can usually find a form listed under Media & PR Resources or their Contact page. They'll ask for some basic information, like the name of your podcast and the size of your audience. Be honest. Even big conventions will consider giving a smaller podcast press credentials. If you can point to content you've created at smaller conventions, it might offset low numbers, since they know they can count on you to help spread the word about their convention to your particular niche.

If you can't land that big interview, you can still get some great content while attending a convention. Go to a panel covering your topic, then approach your fellow fans at the back of the room to ask if they'd like to speak to you. If you're on a panel, record it with your digital recorder, then post it as a special episode. Document your adventure at the convention, describing the relevant sights and sounds for your listeners who couldn't attend. Shoot a vlog for your Facebook page or YouTube channel. Arrange a meetup with your listeners, then interview them. They'll love hearing themselves on the podcast, not to mention meeting their favorite podcast hosts!

But you're going to land that interview, because you followed the rules and took your time building a relationship before making your big "ask."

Conducting A Successful Interview

> "I had the publicist for Brainchild who talked to me, and we had the producer and creator of the show on, and she goes 'Everyone I bring you just loves talking with you.' It's like a dinner party, or that's how we try to make it feel. They get to know, like, and trust you and feel like they can talk to you. That's the thing. You're giving them a platform, but you're giving it to them on your terms." - Michael Dolce , Host - Secrets of the Sire

Conducting an interview with somebody you look up to is scary, even when you're just a casual fan of their work. Then again, you might feel like you know this person intimately, even though they only just heard about you. You want to prepare, execute, and publish a great celebrity interview, but you can't control how your guest reacts. What you can control is you, and by following the tips below, you'll set yourself up for a successful interview your listeners (old and new) will gobble up.

Before The Interview

Research

Homework? Again? Yes, indeed. But the hard work is already done.

If you're a fancaster, you already have an encyclopedic knowledge of the setting, plot, and characters. This gives you an advantage over other interviewers, many of whom have, at most, watched a screener. Depending on their job, you might even know more about the show than the person you're interviewing.

When it comes to research, focus your attention on the person's life and career. You'll be able to think up a million questions about their current gig during the interview, but your guest might not be able to answer those questions without giving something away. I don't recommend asking questions about gossip surrounding the show or the celebrity. Hit up Wikipedia, or Google past interviews to find out what parts of their personal back story they're comfortable discussing.

Write open-ended questions that give your interviewee the chance to talk about everybody's favorite subject: themselves. When we interviewed Victoria Cartagena from *Gotham*, I found out Vicky was from Philadelphia, so I asked her about her favorite hometown pizza place. What followed was a great anecdote from Vicky about her neighborhood pizza shop's radio jingle, and why she doesn't do musicals. Vicky's passion for pizza made her feel more human and three dimensional, which should be one of your goals when interviewing a celebrity or creative professional.

> "I was at San Diego Comicon, and the actors just get asked the same questions over and over again. If you ask something outside the box, they'll appreciate being able to go off-script and have a real human conversation with you." Morgan Glennon, Host - Supergirl Radio/Legends of Tomorrow Podcast

Think of late night talk shows like *The Tonight Show* or *The Late Show*. Sure, Tom Cruise will talk about the cool stunts he performed in *Mission Impossible 17: The Possible Mission*, but that's not the clip you're going to see all over your Facebook feed the next morning. It's the anecdote about Tom running into a fan at Starbucks or some other silly thing. Fans love stories that humanize people they admire, as long as the story doesn't cast the interviewee in a bad light.

The Comedy Central prank show *Nathan For You* did an episode called "The Anecdote" where the host, Nathan Fielder, crafted the perfect talk show anecdote. I encourage watching the entire episode, or at least the clip of the final anecdote from *Jimmy Kimmel Live*, to learn more about the elements that make up a great talk show anecdote. Craft your questions to lead your guest to those key elements.

Outside Voices

As discussed in earlier chapters, you can't go wrong by including a wide range of voices in your podcast. This doesn't stop with cast and crew interviews. You're being granted access to people other fans would love to talk to. Act as their proxy by asking them to submit questions, then use them some in your interview.

The first place you should go to for questions is your listeners. If you have enough lead time, put out a call for questions during your podcast. If you have less lead time, solicit questions on your social media pages. This also builds up excitement for the interview among your audience, ensuring that the interview will be among the most listened to and talked about episodes you record.

"You can share your show on social media and online forums, but be careful, because folks are very protective about their communities. The last thing you want to do is jump in as a new member and make a post like 'Hey, I have a podcast and come listen to me.' That will get you in deep trouble really fast. If you're going to get involved in these communities, join them and offer comments that have nothing to do with your podcast at all. Earn some cred, and then find a way to promote your podcast organically." Kevin Bachelder, Host - Tuning Into SciFi TV

An interview is an opportunity to attract new listeners. Find places online where fans gather to discuss your topic. Most TV shows and movie franchises have a dedicated forum on Reddit, for example. Find and join Facebook Groups that discuss your topic. Post a pic to Instagram promoting the interview, with all the appropriate hashtags. Looking outside of the community you've already built helps grow that community. Offering an exclusive, interactive interview is a great way to get new people listening. Introduce yourself, explain your show and your upcoming interview, then ask people what they'd like to know.

Not every question is a keeper. To be honest, most of them won't be keepers. Some will, and if you use them, make sure you give proper credit during the interview. Nothing will earn you a devoted listener faster than teaching somebody's favorite actor their name.

I look for trends to narrow down question submissions. If five people want to know about the actress's mutant zombie makeup, I prepare my own question about mutant zombie makeup, then give those five people credit when I ask it. If the group is smaller, take the time to call each one of them out by name. For five people or more, I'd just mention that a lot of people asked about it. You'll prove to the newcomers that they'll have the ear of their favorite artists if they join your community, while encouraging your existing listeners to contribute more.

Technical Issues

WARNING: I know I said I wouldn't get technical in this book, but this point is so important to a successful interview I must get into the nitty-gritty.

There's nothing more embarrassing than running into technical issues while you're recording your podcast, doubly so if you're streaming it live to Twitch or YouTube. The worst, though, is when you run into issues in front of an esteemed guest. It makes you look unprofessional, unprepared, and unappreciative of the time they have so graciously donated to you and your listeners.

> "For our first live streamed event, we had tech troubles for the first hour. Our first guest went to lunch and when she came back, we were still having issues. Finally, we get everything set up, start the stream, then proceed to interview folks for the next 3 hours. When I get home, (I see) the stream didn't work. Thankfully I recorded everything, but the whole time we're acting like we're live. It's the reason we don't currently stream." - Nathan Beatty, Host, Creativity in Progress

Don't leave anything to chance. If you're recording over Skype, Zoom, or another online service, do a test recording with a friend to make sure your entire production chain is in order, then **don't touch anything until you record your interview**. It's easy to tweak a volume knob or run a scan that reboots the machine by mistake and mess up all your settings. I never risked it.

When we interviewed Vicky and her co-star Andrew Stewart-Jones for *Legends of Gotham*, we were lucky enough to arrange a test call with each of them earlier in the day, where we all joined a Google Hangout and talked for a few minutes to make sure everything worked. I'm sure part of the reason they gave us the additional time was because we were live streaming, and they knew we wouldn't have time to troubleshoot during the show. Even if you aren't live streaming, it doesn't hurt to ask. A test call with a friend is good, but a test call with the actual person and equipment you'll be recording with is better.

I strongly encourage you to make a backup recording, just in case your primary recording fails. There is no worse feeling as a podcaster than hanging up with a guest, only to discover a great episode was lost because your recorder crashed when you went to export.

Assuming you're making a local recording in Audacity, Audition, or a cloud service like ZenCaster, you have one recording already.

If you're live streaming to a service like Twitch, that's another recording, but it isn't reliable. Live streaming quality is dependent on a million factors outside of your control, and unless your chat room gets your attention, you won't even know something went wrong.

Some VOIP/video chat services like Skype have call recording built into the program. If you use one as your backup, make sure at least one of your copies is recording to a separate hard drive. During one of our early live streams I recorded audio and video to one hard drive and fried it. Hard drives are faster than ever, but they are only so fast, and recording audio and/or video takes a lot of computing power. If you save both copies to one drive and that drive fails, you'll lose the interview.

Prepare for the worst possible scenario by picking up a cheap **Zoom H1n Recorder** ($119 on Amazon) to hook up to your mixing board. This is a battery powered device, so even if you lose power, you won't lose your recording. The input is a 3.5 mm basic headphone jack. If you use a mixing board or audio interface, you can pick up a **male-to-male 3.5 mm** cord to run the audio from your board's headphone jack into the recorder's input. You might need a 1/4 inch adapter, depending on your board's headphone jack. Plug your headphones into the other side of the recorder so you can hear. You can also run audio from the speaker ports on your mixer using a **3.5 mm to dual 1/4 inch** cable like this, which converts the Left/Right speaker channels into one 3.5 mm jack you plug into the recorder.

Make It Fun

If you're interviewing a performer, you'd be a fool to let them get away before giving them a chance to perform. A quick game livens up a long interview, while giving your guest a chance to show off their natural charm and sense of fun.

Gotham's Andrew Stewart-Jones, cracking up about the Condiment King.

It's easy to build a game around your favorite show or movie. For example, when we interviewed Vicky and Andrew for *Legends of Gotham*, we asked them to improvise how their characters would respond to the cheesiest Batman villains like Condiment King, The Flower Gang, and The Dodo Man in a game called "How MCU Are You?". You can see the game doc we created here[14]. We gave them a plausible fan fiction scenario for their character, and then let them go to town. Andrew thought we said "Condom King" instead of "Condiment King," which sent him into a laughing fit, the highlight of the night.

If you're stuck coming up with game ideas, listen to Comedy Bang Bang, Night Attack, or It's All Been Done Podcast for some solid examples of how to play around with your guests.

---

[14]

https://docs.google.com/document/d/14oKr1jS2x5aJncdN Hs0KipvdQvp1dVDA95xwd7ePF-o/edit?usp=sharing

During The Interview

It's 4:00 PM, time to call your interviewee on Skype. You're nervous. It's natural. After all, you're one bad question or one misplaced laugh away from offending somebody whose work you talk about every week. But you've reached the point of no return. This big interview is about to go from "What if?" to "So, that happened," and you worry that it won't go just the way you've planned it in your head.

I've got some good news for you. It won't go just the way you planned it in your head. No use worrying about that. All you can do is prepare, then do your best to keep up with the strong personality joining you for a chat.

Fanning Out

I love how passionate you are about your podcast and whatever it is you talk about. The person you're interviewing loves that too, or else they wouldn't have agreed to be on your show. At the same time, no matter how passionate they are about their current project, to them, it's still a job. Oftentimes, you're asking them about work they did months or years ago.

I get it. You've spent a lot of time thinking about this person's work, and your listeners have detailed questions about timelines. It's going to get geeky, so you need to give your guest context before asking a geeky question.

It's a friendly reminder to both them and your listeners, who don't all watch every episode four times like you do.

Consider your guest's job on the show. If you're talking to an actor, don't ask them why a favorite character had to die. That's a question for a writer or showrunner. Similarly, don't ask crew members for inside dirt about the actors on the show. Pros don't gossip in public, because they like to work. Besides, you wouldn't want anybody to get in trouble for talking to you.

Be Prepared, Remain Flexible

If you did your prep work, you'll feel confident going into your interview. All you have to do is read from your Show Doc and you'll be fine.

But it's hard to keep your cool when the person you talk about talks back to you. You feel yourself getting panicked. You're breathing too loud. Did your guest notice? Then, your voice cracks. Damn it.

Remember, in those nervous moments, all you need to do is ask a question. You have a pro on the other end of the line. Ask them a good question, then sit back and let them drive. You might even have a list of questions right in front of you. Just read one.

There. Now the conversation is going somewhere again. Your guest tells a charming story about her audition, which dovetails into another story about her first meeting with her co-star/love interest. You're still nervous, and you miss her teasing a funny story about a prank she pulled on set.

After you ask your guest a question, it's important that you listen to them and give them your full attention. Many of your guests are trained on how to give a good interview, but their training is dependent on you picking up their cues. Any detail your guest gives you voluntarily is an invitation to ask a follow-up question, unless you agreed not to discuss the topic beforehand. If they don't want to talk about it, they'll let you know. If you're streaming live, just apologize and move on. If you're pre-recording, I'd suggest editing the false start out of the final podcast, since it will just frustrate listeners. In some cases, it might even make them view your guest in a bad light.

In my favorite interviews, I only ask a few of the questions I have written down. If you stay flexible and listen to your guest, the interview can go wonderful places you never expected. When an interview becomes an organic conversation, your listeners will feel more connected to their favorite thing, your guest, and your podcast. They'll feel surprised and delighted, and they'll reward you for it.

Getting Personal

Your listeners are excited for your interview because they want to get to know your guest better, but how personal should you get?

Search for old interviews on Google News or the artist's personal website. You'll get a decent idea how personal they're willing to go in an interview. Don't assume just because they discussed their troubled childhood with Time Magazine, that they'll be comfortable discussing it with you. On the other hand, if they post a Twitter thread about their childhood and the charity it inspired them to create, consider yourself safe to ask more questions. If you see some photos of them drunk on a subway posted by TMZ, keep it to yourself. They probably don't want to talk about it with you, and if they do they'll bring it up.

Whether your interview is video or audio-only, pay strict attention to your guest to make sure they're comfortable. If they get quiet, sound angry, or give you gruff replies, there's a good chance you've crossed a line and made them uncomfortable. Steer the conversation back to a safe topic, or you might lose your guest, and access to future guests.

Everybody should walk away from your interview happy. You, your guests, their people, and your listeners. Go all "Barbara Walters" on them and get a big emotional reaction if you want, but you risk alienating everybody I listed above. If you want official support for your podcast, do your damnedest to make sure nobody regrets getting interviewed by you.

After The Interview

If your guest has time, check in with them after you stop recording to make sure they are 100% okay with how the interview went. If they have any concerns, be sure to hear them out and work with them on edits that will make them more comfortable. Make sure you thank them, and let them know how much their involvement means to you and your listeners. Again, you want your guest to walk away happy, because if they aren't happy, they won't share your episode, and you'll lose out on the promotional juice and increased credibility a high-profile guest offers.

After you hang up, reach out to their people and thank them for the opportunity. If they ask, let them listen to your podcast before you release it. Otherwise, thank them and let them know you'd love to work together to arrange another interview in the future. Tell them you'll follow up when the episode is released.

> "(On online forums), wait for your opportunity. If someone asks about such-and-such a character that you've done interviews with the people, that's when it's time to go 'Oh, we talked to them last week. Here's a link.' Make it real. Don't make it look like the 'Hey, me' syndrome, because that can get you in trouble real fast." Kevin Bachelder, Host - Tuning Into SciFi TV

We created this promotional image as a YouTube thumbnail for the clip, but also used it on social media whenever Gotham's MCU showed up in an episode.

Once everybody is happy with the interview and you release it, circle back around to the forums where you asked for questions and let them know the episode is up. Tag your guest on every social platform you can, as well as the official accounts for their project (main account, writers room, etc.). This is a showcase episode, so don't be afraid to get loud about it. Pull quotes from the interview for social graphics. Clip out key segments and post them to your YouTube channel. Whatever you do to announce a normal episode, do twice as much for this one.

If you spread the word, and conduct a good interview, you will see an increase in downloads and engagement, not only on the current episode, but for your entire back catalog of podcasts. Interviews are the quickest way to grow your listener base, and nothing gives your podcast more credibility than a great interview with a big guest.

T his isn't a technical manual.

If this was a technical manual, this chapter would be about bit rates and audio codecs and pitting podcast hosting services against each other in a fight to the death. For a more technical conversation about hosting and publishing a podcast, the Audacity wiki[15] is a great starting point.

15

https://wiki.audacityteam.org/wiki/How_to_publish_a_Po dcast

I'll share a few pieces of our publishing process I think you'll find useful. These tools will help you increase the quality, utility, and searchability of your podcast with a minimum effort on your part. Content is still king, but there is a lot of content out there. With light editing to give it a professional polish and smart publishing practices, your show will stick out and get noticed.

Editing Tricks

> "We might produce three hours of content for every hour-long show." Darrell Darnell, Co-Founder - Golden Spiral Media

Once you have your podcast recorded, you'll put the raw recording through some process before you publish it. Maybe you record your theme song and other incidental sound cues live, so it's as simple as trimming the ends and exporting your MP3. Maybe you meticulously edit your audio, every person on their own track, with audio clips from the show added in post-production.

As I mentioned earlier, we published our podcasts within 28 hours of an episode airing, so I didn't have time for a lot of post-production. Instead, I developed the following tricks to give our shows a lot of polish in a small amount of time.

Track Edits As You Go

While we usually tried to record all our podcasts "live-to-tape," on occasion we'd record something we'd rather not have in the show. Sometimes it was a curse word. Other times it was an argument with my co-host that got awkward, and not in a good way. Whatever your bad moment is, you aren't going to want to spend time hunting it down when you go to publish the episode.

I have two different ways to track edits. Both use the time code on your recording. This is the number constantly going up as you record, like **_00:02:20.364_**. This breaks down to **HOURS:MINUTES:SECONDS.MILLISECONDS**. If you make a mistake, take note of the time code so you can quickly edit it out in post. Sometimes, I typed time codes into the top of the Show Doc. Other times, I would keep a notepad nearby and jot them down[16]. Keeping track of these time codes saved me time that would have otherwise been spent scrubbing through my timeline to locate mistakes I only half-remembered. I also didn't have to worry about missing something. Once I made it through the list, I knew the show was good to go.

Pro Tip: If you're working from a list, move through the list from the bottom up. If you edit out mistakes that occur earlier on your timeline first, you'll throw off the time codes for the rest of your edit list. Working back-to-front ensures you won't create new problems for yourself.

Bonus Clips

---

[16] Your recording program might have a quick key to add a marker to your timeline, but if you're switching back and forth between your Show Doc, a chat room. and your recording software, it's easy to miss a marker because you hit the quick key to make a marker with another window selected.

I added a little blooper clip at the end of every podcast we published, a reward for listeners who stuck through to the end of the closing theme song. Sometimes it was as simple as some pre-show banter, other times we'd end up improvising a parody of Bad Romance, all about the love life of Emma Swan on *Once Upon A Time*.

These bonus clips can come from your edit list above, provided you're comfortable sharing them. I always hit record 3-5 minutes before we started the actual episode, and we'd often say something silly enough to make the blooper reel while we were getting ready to go live. Since we live streamed our podcasts, we'd often hang out for a few minutes after the official end of the episode and interact with the chat room. I'd keep the recording going, and pull bloopers from there as well.

> "I've listened to shows that are so heavily edited (ahhhs and ummms) out, the people sound unnatural because it takes away their speaking patterns, or else they take out every pause... It doesn't give the audience time to process points because there are no breaks to process what the hosts are saying." Hope Mullinax, Jaig Eyes And Jedi, Geeky Girl Experience.

Truncate Silence

In podcasting, it pays to think before you speak. Collecting your thoughts reduces confusing language, verbal pauses (Umms, Ahhs), and showcases exactly how much of a fancasting pro you are. When your audience can see you, these pauses feel natural because they see your brow furrowing in thought. If they can't see you, they might think something is wrong with their podcast player, or get bored after a few dozen pregnant pauses.

In YouTube videos, vloggers pick up the pace by cutting out awkward silences with *jump cuts*. You can do the same thing for your entire hour-long podcast in just a few clicks using the free audio software Audacity and its built-in effect Truncate Silence, which detects areas of your recording where nobody is talking, then makes them shorter. This can reduce the length of your podcast by up to 5%, so your listeners don't have a chance to get bored.

If you didn't record your podcast in Audacity, export a WAV file from whatever program you use to edit. When it's finished, consider running it through Levelator, which we'll cover in a minute. Import it into Audacity. Hit **Ctrl + A** on your keyboard to select your entire recording, then select **Truncate Silence** under the **Effect** menu.

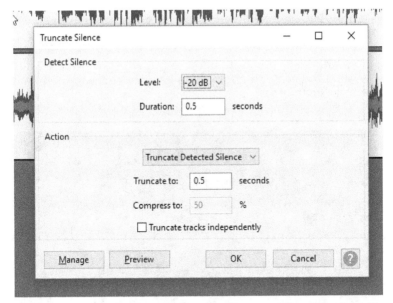

Audacity's Truncate Silence effect, with the default settings.

For the most part, I find the default settings do the job. Run it with the default settings, then play back a minute or two to make sure it doesn't clip out any of the speech. If it does, adjust the Level in the effect settings (above) to allow for a lower threshold. If this doesn't help, you need to normalize your audio with a tool like Levelator before using Truncate Silence.

Levelator

Keeping the loudness of your podcast consistent gives your listeners a better experience, particularly when you have multiple/remote hosts with different recording setups. Nobody wants to have to constantly adjust the volume while listening to a podcast, fumbling to turn it down when the music kicks in, then turning it back up to hear a voicemail.

The Levelator.

Most audio editors have some tool to normalize your audio, but I like a free tool from The Conversation Network called The Levelator. Download and install it from their website, then open it up and drag a WAV file of your podcast onto the Levelator window. Give it a minute to do its thing, and when it's done you'll find a second WAV in the same folder as your original with **_output** added to the end of the filename (ex. MyPodcast.wav > MyPodcast_output.wav).

Rebecca.wav   Rebecca.output.wav

*The "Levelated" file is the one on the right, with **output** in the file name.*

This output file has had all of its audio levels normalized, and will play at a consistent level throughout the podcast. Convert this WAV file into an MP3 and your podcast is ready to publish.

Creating Useful Show Notes

So, you've created a solid hour of audio content. Great work! Now you need to make sure people can find it. Since Google still doesn't have audio search, you'll want to include as much information as possible in your Show Notes, or the blog post attached to your episode that shows up in a podcast player. The more detailed you make your Show Notes, the easier people will be able to find your podcast, and the more value you'll add for your existing listeners.

But what should you include in your show notes?

(S03E13) – Will the Jerome cult seduce a whole city? Dwight takes the stage but his face isn't pretty. Will Penguin maintain his control over Gotham? With Ed killing gangsters his chance isn't awesome. Does Jerome forgive Dwight? Dwight makes a good case. Would any excuse repair a cut face? Why staple your visage before you clean it? You'll get infected once you "Smile Like You Mean It".

Show Notes

Look at this Joker!

Sign up for our newsletter

The Gotham Sweethearts Giveaway – Win A FREE Gotham Action Figure

No Man's Land

"Smile Like You Mean It" Ratings

"Turn That Frown Upside Down" Promo

Upcoming Episode Titles

Bill's Twitter

Anne Marie's Twitter

Join our Community

Support us on Patreon

Legends of Gotham Facebook Group

Contact Us:

E-mail: legendsofgotham@gmail.com
Twitter: http://twitter.com/LegendsOfGotham
Facebook: https://www.facebook.com/groups/LegendsOfGotham
Voicemail Number: (424) 274-2352

An example of our show notes from Legends of Gotham

Episode/Title Description

At the bare minimum, write a short paragraph to let listeners know what you discussed in the podcast. We would generally use our rhyming episode summaries, along with the show's episode title and official numbering. We always used the same episode numbering as pirated content to increase the searchability (i.e. Season 2, Episode 5 is written as 'S02E05').

Here's an example from Legends of Gotham:

> Gotham (S03E12) "Ghosts" – How often does love turn into hate? When Jim killed Lee's husband, he sealed his fate. Once someone dies, do they leave completely? They might still visit at night, discreetly. Is Jerome the messiah? He'd laugh if you asked him. Will Gotham fall to the cultists who've backed him? Will Maria bring trouble to her stately hosts? The past comes alive thanks to Gotham's "Ghosts".

This paragraph should let viewers know at a glance what episode we were covering. I also stuffed it with keywords like characters, locations, and plot points from the episode. If somebody searched for "Lee's husband dies on Gotham" or "Gotham Season 3 Jerome," our podcast would most likely pop up in their search results.

Use this paragraph, and this paragraph only, for the "Short Description" field when you upload your podcast.

You'll also use it to start your "Long Description" later on.

If you're fancasting about a TV show, include at least the episode number, if not the official title, in the Title field. This will make it easier for listeners to browse your back catalog to find your discussion about a particular episode. For example, the episode above was titled Legends of Gotham #93 – (S03E12) Donald J. Penguin.

Links

Links make the web go 'round, and you should include any and all relevant links in your Long Description/Show Notes. Here are just a few examples of links you should include in your Show Notes:

- Your show's social accounts
- Your personal social accounts
- Supporting research (articles, screenshots, etc.)
- News stories
- Episode promos
- Ways to support the show (Patreon, sponsors, etc.)

Always make sure to double-check your links, particularly if you copy and paste them week-to-week. If a viewer wants to support you on Patreon, you don't want to send them to a trailer on YouTube.

Listener Feedback

Include your show's contact information, like your voicemail number and e-mail address, in the Show Notes so users can send feedback when they have something to say. People are way more likely to respond to you if they can do it with just a few clicks in their podcast app.

Some podcasts include every piece of listener feedback they receive in their Show Notes to add more keywords for SEO. We never felt the need to do this, but when the amount of listener feedback for *Greetings From Storybrooke* became overwhelming, we started cutting the feedback we'd read on the show in half. We used half of it on the show, then published a special blog post on our site with our responses to the other half. We'd link to the podcast episode in the blog post, and we'd link to the blog post in the episode's show notes. This gave us nearly the same SEO advantage as putting listener feedback in the Show Notes themselves, but didn't clutter them up and risk breaking our podcast feed with a bunch of HTML formatting. It also let us respond to every listener without hurting the flow of the show. Our listeners felt like their feedback mattered every week, even if it didn't make the final cut.

Promoting Your Episode

Once you publish your episode, let people know. Try these promotional techniques that consistently worked for us.

Episode Posters

Episode posters make your podcast look pro. Most podcast hosting services have a place to upload a custom graphic for the episode. This shows up in podcast players, smart speakers, and even on in-car displays if they listen on the road. It lets podcasters bundle topical branded imagery with their episodes.

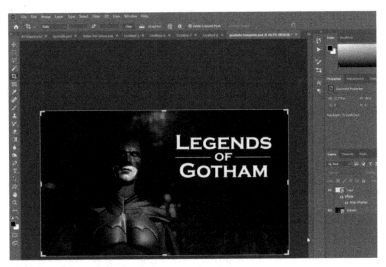

Our template for Legends of Gotham.

I suggest creating a template in Photoshop for your episode poster. Include your podcast logo/album art and a place to drop in topical imagery, like an official promo photo.

Create your episode posters in two different sizes, geared towards different platforms:

- Widescreen (Twitter, Facebook, YouTube, Blog Post)
    - Aspect Ratio: 16x9
    - Resolution: 1920px x 1080px
- Square (Instagram, Episode Thumbnail)
    - Aspect Ratio: 1x1
    - Resolution: 1080px x 1080px

If you don't have access to Photoshop, or don't know how to use it, there are a multitude of apps for this on mobile. Adobe Spark lets you import high-res transparent PNG versions of your podcast logo and build your own templates. Canva has both free and paid options with templates for most social media sites. Built-in image editors for Instagram, Twitter, and Snapchat all have their own unique functionality. Play around with some different free and paid options from the App Store and find a tool that works for you.

TV networks and movie studios send out high-quality promotional photos with their press releases. Some fancasts are lucky enough to be on the press release list and get unfettered access. Lucky them! For the rest of us, many sites post press releases in full, including the high-quality imagery. While I can't provide any legal council, none of my shows, nor any shows made by the fancasters I know, have ever recieved a legal summons/cease and desist/scary letter from a corporate legal team. I assume you'll be okay as long as you use their official promotional materials. Just do a search for your thing + promo pics (ex. "Gotham s03e05 + promo pics", which brings up several links to the photos).

You could also screencap your own stills from an OTT service like Hulu. Fair warning, doing this got our YouTube thumbnails flagged once or twice for copyright. If you want to roll the dice, Greenshot is a fantastic screenshot program that you can also use to edit your episode poster, no Photoshop required!

Social Promotion

With two versions of your episode poster in hand, you're ready to promote your show on multiple social platforms. Write a post promoting your episode when you publish it. If you publish late at night, schedule another post for around 10:00 AM ET the next morning to catch people on both coasts early in the day. We always created a post for the late afternoon or early evening to catch people just getting home from the office.

If you cover a weekly show, always post a link to your latest podcast the day the next new episode releases. Consider posting several, with all the appropriate hashtags, as your show will always have the most social buzz on the day a new episode airs.

Posting this one more time before it becomes irrelevant. #Gotham #GothamMonday
http://t.co/pOGFKg6Bsj

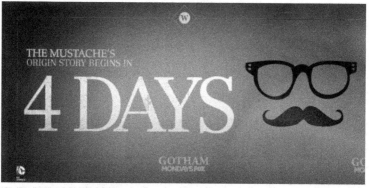

Mon Sep 22 12:54:46 +0000 2014

Our original #GothamMonday tweet, a parody of the social graphics FOX was using to promote the show before the premiere.

Consider making an hourly post on the day a new episode airs. We began publishing official promo pics with snarky comments using the hashtag #GothamMonday a few weeks before *Gotham* premiered. Within a few months, the hashtag we created trended every Monday night and was used by the official accounts for the show as well as the cast. Even when the show moved to Thursdays, we still saw #GothamMonday tweets come through.

"I always try to be available to listeners on social media. If they have a question, if they want to point something out to me, I'm always there to listen. In general, I think our listeners are awesome, impressive and really, really funny. I always like hearing from them, and I make sure to point that out on the podcast and then live it out in the world of social media." Morgan Glennon, Host - Supergirl Radio/Legends of Tomorrow Podcast

The most important social promotion you can do for your podcast doesn't involve links to your podcast. Live tweet an episode. Search show-related hashtags using a tool like Best-Hashtags.com, then respond to random users using the hashtags. Create polls for your followers to rate their favorite characters. Create silly show-related memes. Actively engage with your fellow fans. That's the best way to build a following, so that when you do tweet out those podcast links, you'll have an instant audience of potential new listeners who are one click away from joining your community.

WHEN YOU FALL OUT OF LOVE WITH THE SHOW

"Podcasting is work. Editing, web site, doing it when you aren't having a good week... It's a lot of work, so be ready to put some time in. But, that passion covers it all. As long as you've got that, man, you're probably going to be golden." Kevin Bachelder, Host - Tuning Into SciFi TV

I t's hard to admit when it's over.

In 2016, after podcasting about *Once Upon A Time* for nearly four years, my co-host Anne Marie and I decided to end our first podcast, *Greetings From*

Storybrooke. The "Land of Untold Stories" arc was our breaking point. After two seasons of being excited by the concepts *Once* was exploring, we were over feeling disappointed by the execution. We'd had enough. If the section on *Building A Show* gave you any indication, we spent a lot of time planning our podcasts. After Season 5, we agreed that the show just wasn't worth the time to us any more, particularly when we were finding so much success and fulfillment with *Legends of Gotham*.

Don't get me wrong. It was a hard decision to end our podcast while *Once* was still airing new episodes. It felt like throwing a dinner party, then pushing all the guests out the door halfway through the night because you want to go to sleep. It felt like quitting, and I don't like being a quitter.

> *"I used to write recaps for 'The Walking Dead,' and in the second and third season, I really stopped enjoying watching 'The Walking Dead.' It was a conflict for me, because I liked interacting with the fans about it. I liked writing about it. I just hated the show, and I felt bad that I couldn't write honestly about what I was seeing. All of a sudden the comments went from 'Hey, we're having a good time with "The Walking Dead"' to 'Why are you picking on "The Walking Dead" for*

several hundred words?"' Justin Robert Young, Host - Who's The Boss?

Looking back on it, quitting was the kindest thing we could have done for our listeners. Some of them were already complaining we were too negative about the show. That started shortly after the ninth episode of Season 5, "The Bear King." We disliked the *Brave* crossover episode so much that we very loudly refused to discuss it, pretending that it hadn't aired in the United States, and that some of our listeners had watched a "Canadian Bootleg" of the episode.

GREETINGS FROM STORYBROOKE
#147 - (S05E08) "Birth"

AmyP they are in denial lol
Kastor LOL the denial of this mystery second episode is hilarious.

Our chat room took this in good stride, but it was the beginning of the end.

We referred to "The Bear King" as The Canadian Bootleg from then on, and it definitely cost us a few listeners, which bums me out. I see now our frustration with the show was dripping out in jokes that went too far and revealed too much about how we really felt about *Once*.

We could have continued talking about *Once* for two more seasons, but if we couldn't maintain our *Café POV*, how many listeners would we have left by the time *Once* finally wrapped? Listening to two people talk about how they can't believe a show hasn't been canceled yet doesn't make for a compelling podcast, and it doesn't provide anything positive for anybody. No. Better to end it while our listeners still liked us, then become the target of a Oncer hashtag on Twitter. Those Oncers were intense.

AmyP lol
AmyP me too Dawn
ThisIsHope Pour one out for Gus Gus because Johanna did it!

Our last episode of Greetings, complete with plenty of inside jokes in the chat room.

We decided to quit *Greetings From Storybrooke* several weeks before the *Once* season finale, which gave us time to enjoy and say goodbye to our listeners. Our final episode, "Farewell From Storybrooke," featured a long discussion about the season finale, followed by an even longer Feedback segment and closing thoughts from us. Everybody said what *Greetings From Storybrooke* meant to them, including *Once Upon A Time* actor Jarod Joseph.

"Caught wind that you kids were closing down the shop and I just had to reach out and wave a verbal goodbye, if you will. Pour one out for the little guy Gus Gus one more time. Goose Goose if ya' nasty. Bill, Anne Marie, thanks for the rapport. Love begets love and I love you guys." - **Jarod Joseph**, Billy The Mechanic/Gus Gus on Once Upon A Time

"Sad to hear that @GFStorybrooke is ending their podcast. You guys ran a great podcast that was always fun to listen to and got me into the Once fandom. You were one of the first podcasts I ever listened to, and my first internet friends." - Marshall

"Robin Hood dying did not make me as sad as you guys becoming disenchanted and throwing in the towel." - @mystickid

"Oh my god! My heart is breaking." - Liz

"Well, there goes my final reason to keep watching Once Upon A Time. I was hanging in just so I could follow your podcast." - Amelia

"You two always brought the fun of Once Upon A Time and had the most vibrant group of listeners ever. You should be very proud of what you accomplished (and still are in other podcasts). It was so incredibly awesome to meet you, hang with you and be a part of your panel at Regal Con, Bill. I'll never forget it. You both will be missed, but what you did for Once Upon A Time will never be forgotten. Best wishes and much love to you both." - Jeff Roney, **Once Upon A Time Podcast**

"I want to thank you both for all the years of time and energy you put into entertaining us and giving us all a place to laugh, cry, vent, theorize, and just be crazy fans. The chat room and regular writers and callers like Bobby, Hope and Other Annemarie have made this show even more fun." - Tracey

"I joined the podcast about halfway through Season 2, and I have thoroughly enjoyed it ever since. Even when my enjoyment of the show started to wane in the past season or so, your podcast always made the show more enjoyable to me. Best of luck on your other podcasts, and I'm sure that I'll find one or two of them to listen to!" - Vicki

The comments from our listeners hit me in the gut. I second-guessed our decision at the time, but I think we made the right choice. Some listeners admitted they were only watching *Once* so they could make sense of our podcast. What bigger compliment for a fancaster, that our podcast was so important to them that they continued watching a show they didn't even enjoy anymore, simply because we sat down and talked about it in our home office for an hour and change every week? What an honor for our silly little fancast to have such an impact on so many people.

> "I had to produce a weekly show about The Bachelorette, and I couldn't care less about that show, but I enjoyed producing it because of the passion of the hosts." Darrell Darnell, Co-Founder - Golden Spiral Media

A year later, we shut down *Legends of Gotham, Universe Box News,* and *We're So LOST*, not because we fell out of love, but because we just didn't have the time. I also wanted to try some new podcast formats, ones that weren't subject to the quality of whatever it was I decided to review. The result? My scripted "sketch dramedy" podcast *The Fakist*, which has featured over 100 voices from multiple countries, many of them former listeners to my fancasts. As of this writing, *The Fakist* is about to go into its third and final season. It doesn't get the numbers our fancasts did, but I'm proud of what we've been able to accomplish together over the internet.

The last goodbye on *Legends of Gotham* was definitely easier. While it was still a hard decision, we felt much better leaving *Gotham* while we were still in love with it. It didn't feel like giving up. It felt like moving on to something new.

PASSING THE TORCH

"When we started The Signal, we decided really early on that The Signal would not have 'fans'. We were all fans of Firefly." Les Howard, Host - The Signal

Quitting your podcast, or simply moving on, doesn't mean your podcast needs to end. With the right "Bobbys" in your audience, it's possible to pass the torch over to people who still have a passion for your topic. People who your listeners already know, because they talk to them in the chat room every week.

After ending *Greetings From Storybrooke*, we gave the show to Bobby. Actual Bobby. Not an idealized Bobby. Bobby Hawke, the same guy who left us a voicemail as "Robert From Bradenton."

The idea came up during a Hangout with our Patreon supporters the summer after we quit *Greetings*. We held these Hangouts every month. We'd spend a couple hours drinking, playing games, and generally "hanging out" with our most fervent supporters, the ones who gave us money. Bobby asked us if we'd ever consider bringing back the show. We laughed and laughed and laughed, then realized he was serious and said no. Our longtime listener Elizabeth Plascencia suggested we let our listeners take over the show.

I thought the idea was brilliant. *Greetings* would live on, and see *Once* through its final season! The best part? I wouldn't have to do any of the heavy lifting! It was settled.

I joined Bobby for several Skype calls to help him with all the technical details, and the new *Greetings From Storybrooke* launched on October 22, 2016, about four years and one month after our embarrassing, unprofessional premiere podcast. It featured Bobby Hawke as the host, with Elizabeth Plascencia and Tony Hooper as co-hosts. A few months later, Monica Jones would join them to round off their fearsome foursome. By the time *Once*'s finale aired two years later, they'd produced an additional 37 episodes of the podcast, pushing our final episode count to over 200.

The new crew. Damn, these guys were good.

I did some production work on the new podcast. I'd create the episode posters for Bobby before they recorded. After they were done, I'd pull down the live stream from YouTube, publish it on our YouTube channel, then edit and publish an audio version. It took some time, sure, but nothing like I spent as a host/producer/editor.

If we made one mistake when we ended *Greetings*, it's that we didn't give any indication that the podcast would ever come back. In fact, we said several times in stark terms that it would never come back. When the podcast did come back, many of our former listeners had already unsubscribed. I did what I could to communicate that *Greetings* was publishing new episodes, but Bobby and the gang never saw the levels of engagement we enjoyed, which I know disappointed them. I did what I could to promote their show, up to and including making guest appearances. Their numbers grew, but *Greetings From Storybrooke* never fully recovered from being canceled.

Still, the new *Greetings* gang held together what remained of our community for just a little bit longer. I was a proud Papa, sitting back and watching every episode. At first, I saw them copying what we did, but before long they discovered their own strengths as podcasters and grew the little show we started in our garage into something different and new that I got to enjoy as a fan of *theirs*.

The current and former hosts of Greetings From Storybrooke, hanging out after the season finale. We're only missing Liz.

When *Once Upon A Time* announced its final episode in June of 2018, we invited any of the hosts who could make it to our house in Orlando to watch the finale and do a Facebook Live after it aired. While we hadn't live streamed in months, and were beset with many technical issues, the whole event felt easy-breezey, like a family reunion where the family actually likes each other. Bringing everything to a close, sitting in our home with some of our most passionate and prolific listeners... How beautiful. How poetic. How *right*.

Hanging out with Bobby and Tony at Universal Studios the day after the finale.

If you must quit, I highly suggest asking your listeners if they would like to take over your fancast, preferably before your final episode. I can't put into words how magical it was to see my fairy tale dream live on, long after I woke up and went back to the real world.

NOW GO DO IT!

"Fancasting has opened up an immense world for me of other passionate people. Podcasting has led to so many life-long friendships, and it's been a major confidence-booster for me. I mean, I'm passionate about something and get to talk to other people who are (passionate)." Kevin Bachelder, Host - Tuning Into SciFi TV

I n closing, I'm reminded what an honor it was to serve our listeners for so many years. Being a fancaster taught me who I am, creatively, and gave me dozens of friendships I still nurture to this day. Nothing can ever be like it was, but my listeners still are, and will continue to be, a part of my life for as long as Twitter exists, so like until 2022?

> "You can start a podcast at any time. Some people go week by week as the media airs, speculating as the season progresses. Some people wait until a season is complete to do a full season recap in one episode. There's no one right time to start a podcast. The most important thing is to love and have passion for what you're speaking about." Hope Mullinax, Jaig Eyes And Jedi, Geeky Girl Experience.

Fancasting offers many rewards: Friendships, increased confidence, notoriety, even a little cash here and there. You aren't going to be good when you start. It's going to take trial and error and awkward moments and late nights, but I promise you, it'll be worth it. Even if you fail, hosting a podcast with an active and engaged community will teach you so much about yourself. The best part is, if you plan it right, and don't mind sounding tinny, the initial investment can be as low as $0, which is way cheaper than any cooking class you'll find on Meetup.com.

> "The key was we didn't think we had it right out of the gate. We had to wait and see where it went. Don't wait until you have the perfect set up. Do it." Kevin Bachelder, Host - Tuning Into SciFi TV

You can't buy experience, and you'll need a lot of it. It took us a year of recording *Greetings From Storybrooke* before we were any good at it, and we were both performers already! I've done my best to boil down all the lessons we learned, but you'll learn your own lessons. The most important thing you can do is start. Even if it isn't perfect, even if the only people who listen to your fancast are you and your co-hosts, start now. If you aren't good yet, you need to get good, so when the stars align and people notice your podcast, you'll be ready to show them why they should keep paying attention.

As your show grows and you find your community, don't forget the *Café POV*: Publish consistently, strive to be accurate, be friends with your listeners, expand your show whenever possible, don't be afraid to play around, remain objective and respectful about people's opinions, and give your audience a voice on your show. You'll attract new listeners, and keep the old ones coming back week after week. You owe it to them.

"We always want to be natural. We don't want to force an opinion or go with a script. When we all get on our Skype call to get ready, we purposely don't talk about the show, so when it comes up, it's very natural." Kevin Bachelder, Host - Tuning Into SciFi TV

If there's one regret I have, it's that we planned our podcasts out a little too much. If we weren't careful, we'd ping pong pre-written notes back and forth with little attention to what we actually said to each other. Still, a solid plan will give you confidence when you hit record. Planning isn't a bad thing, but it's important to remain in the moment and flexible for whatever happens on the show. Those spontaneous side jaunts will become classic clips you'll hear about years after you've forgotten them.

I'll always be proud we built a platform that welcomed all voices and opinions. Many of our listeners thought of our show as their show, and it kind of was, sometimes literally. Without the active engagement from our listeners, we would have never known why they liked us, and what they didn't like. Without that information, it would have taken us a lot longer to get good at fan podcasting. Our listeners were contributors to the show, and encouraged new people to get involved. They helped us present the larger picture of the fandom. If you didn't like my opinion, we'd share fifteen other opinions at the end of the episode you might agree with. We taught our listeners how to disagree without being disagreeable.

Getting that official stamp of approval from the project you're reviewing, by way of official interviews, retweets, and swag is exciting. You'll grow your podcast's credibility within your niche, if you don't piss off the talent and get yourself blacklisted. Approach press interviews with all due preparation, but when you get nervous, remember that no matter how important it seems, this interview probably won't make or break your show. Your job is to ask good questions, then let your guest drive. Relax, listen, and enjoy the experience.

Spreading the word about your podcast can feel embarrassing, especially when you do it week after week without seeing noticeable response. But somebody's out there, typing a search into Google to see if anybody else thinks The Bachelor has some interesting things to say about climate change. If your episode comes up in their search, they'll dive in and binge your entire back catalog in a week, then show up in the chat during your next live stream to tell you what you got wrong about Chad's "evening look."

> "Passion is only as important to fancasting as gasoline is important to an automobile." Justin Robert Young, Host - Who's The Boss?

Make your podcast for your listeners, but if you lose your passion for your topic, the best thing you can do for your listeners is to step away. If you're sick of talking about something, nobody else wants to listen to you talk about it either.

If you do decide to step away, it doesn't mean your podcast or community has to die. Pass the torch to the next generation, then watch them grow the show you started into something mostly different, but just as wonderful. Your show exists because you had passion for your topic. If that passion loses its flame, pass on the ember before it burns to ash and you lose it forever.

With this book complete, I've expressed everything I ever wanted to say about fan podcasting. I loved fancasting, but outside of guest appearances on other people's podcast, I probably won't do it again. Then again, never say never...

If there's somebody to blame for me leaving fancasting behind, it's the people who listened to our shows. Our podcasts weren't about *Once Upon A Time* or *Gotham*. We discussed those shows, sometimes over-discussed them, but on a personal level, the podcasts were about learning to trust in the power of friendship to pursue common goals, together.

To that end, in late 2019 I launched a new company called **Do Anything Media**, a virtual playhouse and a sacred creative space to collaborate with other dreamers just like you. We're building platforms for artists to showcase and sell their work. We're producing podcasts, books (like this one), and videos to teach and inspire creative people of all stripes. Most importantly, we're making a community to connect creative people to each other.

As you continue to grow as a creator, I'd like to extend an open invitation to join our Do Anything community. When you visit http://join.doanything.media, you'll be asked to join our mailing list. Punch in your e-mail, and we'll send you some instructions to get started. I'll keep the spam to a minimum.

I've also started a different kind of podcast. *I Made This* (http://imadethis.doanything.media) features interviews with passionate people executing their "Big Ideas" in realistic ways. I've released a ton of great interviews so far, some of which are quoted in this book, and hope to continue talking to cool creative people for as long as I can pay my podcast hosting bill.

Whether you join our community or not, I'm here for you if you have any questions about fancasting, the book, or just need a guest to join you for a riveting discussion about your favorite show. Let me know when you release your first episode too. I'd love to check it out.

Twitter/Instagram: @billmeeks
E-mail: contact@doanything.media

I'm Bill Meeks. Until next time, Greetings from Storybrooke!

Join the Do Anything creative community for access to free podcasts, books, training, and creative community projects you can get involved in. Join us and get unlimited access to the virtual playhouse by visiting http://join.doanything.media.

Sign up, and get a free pack of templates to use for your fancast, including show docs, episode posters, and more.

We can do anything, together.

Show Notes

Much like you'll do for your podcast, we've compiled a list of all the relevant links to resources and examples here at the back of the book for easy reference, organized by chapter.

Foreward

Tuning Into SciFi TV

http://tuningintoscifitv.com/

Relevance: Host Kevin Bachelder is quoted in this chapter for the first time.

Universe Box

http://universebox.com

Relevance: An archive of all the podcasts we produced under the Universe Box banner.

Greetings From Storybrooke

http://links.doanything.media/greetings

Relevance: Our first fancast, about ABC's *Once Upon A Time*.

Legends Of Gotham

http://links.doanything.media/legends

Relevance: Our most popular fancast, about FOX's *Gotham*.

Gotham TV Podcast

http://gothamtvpodcast.com/

Relevance: A competing Gotham podcast we've always been friendly with. Co-host Derek is quoted several times in the book.

The Signal

http://signal.serenityfirefly.com/mmx/

Relevance: Host Les Howard is quoted in this chapter for the first time.

The Audacity to Podcast

https://theaudacitytopodcast.com/

Relevance: A great resource for technical podcast training by Daniel J. Lewis.

PotentialCast: A Buffy The Vampire Slayer Podcast

http://links.doanything.media/potentialcast

Relevance: Host Stephanie Smith is quoted in this chapter for the first time.

I Made This

http://imadethis.doanything.media

Relevance: My new interview podcast. Several quotes in this book are pulled from these episodes.

"How To Start A Fancast" Panel, 2013

http://links.doanything.media/fanpodcastpanel

Relevance: Several quotes in this book are pulled from this panel I hosted at Dragon Con 2013 in Atlanta, GA.

The 3 Rules of Criticism

Supergirl Radio

http://supergirlradio.com/

Relevance: Hosts Rebecca Johnson and Morgran Glennon are quoted in this chapter for the first time.

Goethe's Three Questions

http://links.doanything.media/threequestions

Relevance: Slideshare presentation on Goethe's three questions for critics.

The Café POV

Golden Spiral Media
http://www.goldenspiralmedia.com/
Relevance: Co-founder Darrell Darnell is quoted in this chapter for the first time.

Jaig Eyes And Jedi
http://links.doanything.media/jaigyes
Relevance: Host Hope Mullinax is quoted in this chapter for the first time.

Geeky Girl Experience
https://www.geekygirlexperience.com/
Relevance: Writer Hope Mullinax is quoted in this chapter for the first time.

Bleeding Cool
http://links.doanything.media/richjohnston
Relevance: Head Writer Rich Johnston has a quote in this chapter from his episode of *I Made This*.

Olicity Shipping Wiki
https://shipping.fandom.com/wiki/Olicity
Relevance: Just in case you wanted to know more about Olicity or shipping.

Greetings From Storybrooke #22 - Super Mega Episode

http://links.doanything.media/supermegaepisode

Relevance: One example of when we were late recording an episode and had to double up.

Get In The Mecha

http://campsite.bio/getinthemecha

Relevance: Host Jamal is quoted in this chapter for the first time.

Greetings From Storybrooke #41 - Letters From Storybrooke #1

http://links.doanything.media/supermegaepisode

Relevance: The first in a series of special podcasts we produced so we could get to all the listener feedback.

Secrets of the Sire

https://secretsofthesire.com/

Relevance: Host Michael Dolce is quoted in this chapter for the first time.

The Fringe Podcast

http://www.thefringepodcast.com/

Relevance: Host Darrell Darnell shares an anecdote about a meet-up for listeners of his Fringe podcast.

RhymeZone
https://rhymezone.com/
Relevance: A great rhyming dictionary you can use to create your own rhyming summaries. Also has a ton of tools for writers.

Legends of Gotham #63 - Wrath of the Spoiler Party
http://links.doanything.media/spoilerparty
Relevance: Between seasons we'd hold "Spoiler Party" episodes like this one to report on all the big news without pissing people off. This episode also includes an interview with Executive Producer John Stephens.

People.com > Gotham Costars Morena Baccarin and Ben McKenzie Are Dating
http://links.doanything.media/gothamgossip
Relevance: The story that forced us to establish our editorial policy in regards to relevant gossip.

DCTV Podcasts
http://www.dctvpodcasts.com/
Relevance: A podcasting group devoted to covering TV shows based on DC Comics characters. *Legends of Gotham* was a founding podcast for the network.

Look At This Joker

http://links.doanything.media/lookatthisjoker

Relevance: An archive of the page where we compiled all the material we covered in our "Look At This Joker" segment on *Legends of Gotham*.

Creativity In Progress

https://www.thecipnetwork.com/

Relevance: Host Nathan Beatty is quoted in this chapter for the first time.

Sample Show Doc

http://links.doanything.media/sampleshowdoc

Relevance: A sample show doc from *Legends of Gotham* #94.

Giving Your Listeners A Voice

Bobby Hawke on Twitter

https://twitter.com/InevitableHawke

Relevance: One of our first listeners, who eventually took over our first podcast.

Legends of Gotham #81- Live From Tampa Bay Comicon

http://links.doanything.media/gothambobby

Relevance: A live Gotham panel we invited Bobby to join us on.

Greetings From Wonderland

http://links.doanything.media/wonderland

Relevance: Our short-lived *Greetings From Storybrooke* spin-off about the short-lived *Once Upon A Time* spin-off *Once Upon A Time In Wonderland*.

Legends of Gotham #20 - Podcast Roundtable #2

http://links.doanything.media/roundtable

Relevance: One of many roundtable podcasts we did with other podcasters in our niche.

Greetings From Storybrooke "Once If...?" Specials

http://links.doanything.media/onceif

Relevance: The three "Once If...?" specials we did at the suggestion of our listener Hope Mullinax.

Greetings From Storybrooke #44 - Pirate Shipping
http://links.doanything.media/teambill
Relevance: The episode where we launched a shipping war with #TeamBill and #TeamAnneMarie hashtag battles that went on for years.

Greetings From Storybrooke #45 - Letters From Storybrooke #1
http://links.doanything.media/teamannemarie
Relevance: The episode where our fans responded to our silliness in #44.

Legends of Gotham #69 - Batman v Superman: Dawn of Justice
http://links.doanything.media/batmanvsuperman
Relevance: We had two listeners join us to discuss the film, which related to the show we covered.

Feed The Trolls

Trolling The Trolls

http://links.doanything.media/trolltoys

Relevance: It should be pretty obvious.

Engaging The Cast And Crew

The Gotham Sweethearts Giveaway

http://links.doanything.media/gothampromo

Relevance: A promo we shot to promote our giveaway contest, featuring prizes provided by Diamond Select Toys.

IMDBPro

https://pro.imdb.com/

Relevance: A great resource to look up agents, managers, and publicists to book celebrity interviews.

Greetings from Storybrooke #127 - Live from Regal Con 2015

http://links.doanything.media/greetingspanel

Relevance: I hosted a live *Greetings From Storybrooke* panel at the Regal Con convention in Anaheim, CA in 2015.

Legends of Gotham #13 - (S01E07) All That Zsasz

http://links.doanything.media/montoya

Relevance: A direct link to our "voicemail interview" with Gotham's Victoria Cartagena, which eventually led to her appearing on our podcast for a live episode.

Nathan For You - "The Anecdote"

http://links.doanything.media/anecdote

Relevance: An episode of the Comedy Central series *Nathan For You* which will teach you the types of questions you should ask to get entertaining answers in an interview.

Legends of Gotham #17 - Montoya and Allen Join Us LIVE!

http://links.doanything.media/mcuinterview

Relevance: Victoria Cartagena and Andrew Stewart-Jones joined us, along with the hosts of Gotham TV Podcast, for a fun interview with games, questions, and lots of laughter.

Zoom H1n Recorder

http://links.doanything.media/zoomrecorder

Relevance: The handheld recorder I recommend to make a backup recording of your podcast, very important when you have special guests.

Male-To-Male 3.5mm Cord

http://links.doanything.media/35cord

Relevance: Use this cable to run from your mixer to your recorder.

1/4 Inch Adapter

http://links.doanything.media/quarterinchadapter
Relevance: Another piece of hardware you might need to make a backup recording.

3.5mm To Dual 1/4 Inch Cable

http://links.doanything.media/35toquarter
Relevance: Another piece of hardware you might need to make a backup recording.

How MCU Are You?

http://links.doanything.media/howmcuareyou
Relevance: An example of the type of game you can play with celebrity guests.

How MCU Are You? Game Doc

http://links.doanything.media/samplegamedoc
Relevance: How we prepared for the game.

Comedy Bang Bang

https://www.earwolf.com/show/comedy-bang-bang/
Relevance: A show that has fun with their guests.

Night Attack

https://nightattack.tv/
Relevance: Another show that has fun with their guests.

It's All Been Done

http://www.theorangegroves.com/allbeendone

Relevance: A final show that has fun with their guests.

Publishing Your Podcast

Audacity

https://www.audacityteam.org/

Relevance: The best free audio editing software around. Useful for its Truncate Silence effect.

Truncate Silence - The Audacity Wiki

http://links.doanything.media/truncatesilence

Relevance: Use this to speed up your podcast without listeners noticing.

The Levelator

http://www.conversationsnetwork.org/levelator

Relevance: A great tool that automatically adjusts the volume to consistant levels across your entire podcast.

Adobe Spark

https://spark.adobe.com/

Relevance: A tool you can use to make your episode poster if you don't have Photoshop.

Canva

https://www.canva.com/

Relevance: Another tool for episode posters, with both free and paid plans.

Example Search For Promotional Art

http://links.doanything.media/gothamsearch

Relevance: Here's an example of how I found promo art every week for *Legends of Gotham.*

Greenshot

https://getgreenshot.org/

Relevance: A powerful screenshot and image editing tool that will help you with your posters.

Best-Hashtags.com

http://best-hashtags.com/

Relevance: A hashtag search tool, for hashtags to include in your social posts.

Greetings from Storybrooke #165 - Farewell from Storybrooke

http://links.doanything.media/lastepisode

Relevance: Our last episode of the original *Greetings From Storybrooke*, circa 2016.

Greetings from Storybrooke #147 - One Great Episode

http://links.doanything.media/onegreatepisode

Relevance: The beginning of the end for *Greetings*, when we obnoxiously insisted the *Brave* crossover episode hadn't happened.

Greetings from Storybrooke #148 - The Canadian Bootleg

http://links.doanything.media/canadianbootleg

Relevance: Due to listener outcry, Bobby Hawke volunteered to review The Bear King with his daughter in this special episode.

Once Upon A Time Podcast

http://www.onceuponatimepodcast.com/

Relevance: One of fellow Once Upon A Time podcasters, who wrote in for our last episode.

Universe Box News

http://links.doanything.media/universeboxnews

Relevance: The short-lived reboot of our show *Universe Box*. For some reason we thought we should do a generic entertainment news show. Lesson learned.

We're So LOST

http://links.doanything.media/solost

Relevance: A LOST podcast we did in the summer months when Gotham was off the air. We'd never seen the show, hence we were very lost.

The Fakist

https://thefakist.com

Relevance: What I did after the fancasts. The description reads "Covering the fake news... For Real. Anchors Paul DaFoe and LeAnn Snyder are as devoted to making stuff up as other journalists are to actual journalism. A sketch dramedy that blends topical fake news stories with the ongoing saga of the best fake news team in the business."

Legends of Gotham #102 - A Fitting Finale

http://links.doanything.media/afittingfinale

Relevance: Our last regular episode of *Legends of Gotham* in 2017. We would eventually bring the show back for the last season of *Gotham* in 2019.

Greetings From Storybrooke #167 - The Land of Unreviewed Episodes

http://links.doanything.media/newgreetings

Relevance: The first episode of the *Greetings From Storybrooke* reboot, featuring our listeners as hosts.

Greetings From Storybrooke #0 - Magic Is Coming

http://links.doanything.media/firstgreetings

Relevance: Our first fancast ever, a pilot for our *Once Upon A Time* show. It's pretty rough.

Greetings From Storybrooke #204 - Leaving Storybrooke (Again)

http://links.doanything.media/leavingstorybrooke

Relevance: The final final episode of *Greetings From Storybrooke*, with both generations of hosts joining together to celebrate *Once* and how it brought us all together.

Now Go Do It!
Join Do Anything Media

http://join.doanything.media

Relevance: Join my new company, built on the same sense of creative collaboration as our Universe Box podcast network.

I Made This

http://imadethis.doanything.media

Relevance: My new interview podcast. Several quotes in this book are pulled from episodes.

www.ingramcontent.com/pod-product-compliance
Lightning Source LLC
LaVergne TN
LVHW052058060326
832903LV00061B/3357